SEEDS OF LIBERATION

Spiritual Dimensions to Political Struggle

SEEDS OF LIBERATION

Spiritual Dimensions to Political Struggle

Edited by Alistair Kee

SCM PRESS LTD

334 01489 1
© SCM Press Ltd 1973
First published 1973 by SCM Press Ltd,
56 Bloomsbury Street London
Type set by Gloucester Typesetting Co. Ltd
and printed in Great Britain by
Redwood Press Limited
Trowbridge, Wiltshire

CONTENTS

Viv Broughton
PREFACE

Dear Sir,
I read your manifesto
with great interest
but it doesn't say anything
about singing.   *Adrian Mitchell*

The material contained in this book grew largely out of an extra-ordinary four day gathering held in Huddersfield at the beginning of January 1973. The event was sponsored by the Student Christian Movement in response to a widespread feeling among radical Christians, that a re-examination of our faith – in the context of our more usually articulated political radicalism – was long overdue. The response of the event was an unusual one in that it was not primarily an intellectual response; the re-examination required was not so much a cerebral critique of theology or politics but a flesh and blood discovery of spiritual roots. As John Davies said afterwards, 'the whole gospel of Jesus makes it plain that any spiritual dimension is *primarily* a matter of events and experiences rather than intellectual constructs and propositions'.

For most of the 350 people who took part – many of them students but the ages ranged from four months to sixty years – it proved to be a special, if fleeting, experience of a joyous liberating community.

'. . . most important was the creation of a temporary
revolutionary community, organized unobtrusively and
democratically, with a simple communitarian lifestyle –
and despite overcrowing and chaos, being joyful
TOGETHER . . .'

Colin Archer (*Roadrunner 42*)

It has proved impossible adequately to reflect in the form of this book the substance of the actual event itself. The experiences that could not have been planned and cannot be properly communicated were precisely those features that made the occasion extraordinary. Most often these were experiences of a eucharistic or celebratory nature, but there were other times when a truly remarkable ethos of collective responsibility overtook us. For once, the simple business of looking after each other's needs – usually a delegated or despised activity – was central to the consciousness of a political gathering. Books are designed to communicate other (but not more important) aspects of our existence and we are therefore only able to pass on here some of what is available and possible to print.

This we have collected into three sections. Firstly, the transcripts of the contributions of Alistair Kee, Dan Berrigan, Colin Winter and Jim Forest; secondly, something of the response at the time to the questions raised; and thirdly, reflections on the subject and the implications for any conceivable future. We are fully aware that this is neither all the debate nor the end of it, and in some ways the material here has been overtaken (or perhaps it would be more accurate to say illuminated) by events. Dan Berrigan's vision of the Beast – armed capital, conscripting State, cancerous power complex – that took such a firm hold in collective imagination, dramatically anticipated the incredible sagas of high level corruption that have unfolded since on both sides of the Atlantic. Revalations indeed!

These communications were put together in the hope that whatever may also be unfolding, within the Belly of the Beast, shall flower into liberation and not wither into death.

Viv Broughton

Love, solidarity and deeply affectionate gratitude must go to many who put a part of their lives into this event. In particular we would mention Bob Gallagher, Andrew Cowling, Robert Jones and Gerry Marshall who all worked their hearts out; the *Homeless in Manchester* group for their food and their spirit; Peter Michel for risking his church; Mercia Ernstzen who spent the time in hospital; Helen Duncan at Moss Side Press for once again performing miracles of printing; Rory and the Ceili band for the riots; and Tom McGarth for holding the rings. Mary Condren was involved in the organizing of the conference and without her determination in collecting and transcribing tapes this book could not have appeared.

PART ONE

Is there a Sower in the House?

Alistair Kee
THE CRITICISM OF THE SPIRIT

A new term has entered the vocabulary of politically radical Christians in Britain – spirituality. Willingness to look again at this area, an area previously regarded as alien to activism, reflects the mood of the moment. There is a feeling of exhaustion after a period of frenetic political activity, and at the same time a sense of unease. Many radical Christians left religious institutions for the sake of their souls. They felt the urgency of commitment and found no way of pursuing it within the church or Christian organizations. Nor did they find in traditional spirituality any resources for carrying out their responsibilities in social and political spheres. In the last two years, however, it has become clear that such commitments have not been fully carried through, that there is a hollowness at the centre of political life.

This does not mean that the flight into political struggle was wrong, nor is it to be regretted. Looking back, it is difficult to see what was the alternative. And there were many benefits. False barriers were broken down between radical Christians and other radicals. There was a solidarity of those who looked for change and were willing to take responsibility for it. Christians gained an analysis of what is and a vision of what might be. They worked with others who walk by faith and continue in hope. In the uniting of ideas and experience they were politicized and given a new perspective on their world.

Christian faith should have given such a perspective, but for the most part provided no alternative to the conventional wisdom of the culture. The received faith prohibited things more trivial than evil and distracted from things which should never have been allowed to exist. It was about a new life which was never exhibited, about power which was never used to recreate the world. The old spirituality too often described a world which radical Christians could not inhabit and fitted them only too well for the life of this world and a world to come. Christian faith was frustrating because it demanded nothing that really mattered; disappointing, since nothing was promised that

3

was worth having; disillusioning, since all was described and nothing changed.

They did not turn away from Christian faith, but it was difficult to see how it had any bearing on political struggle. If the connection were not simply to be romantic or nostalgic, what was the contribution of faith to struggle? It looked as if Christian faith must be left behind, but increasingly there has been experienced a hollowness at the centre of political life; the struggle has run into continuing and fundamental problems. Even some of the most able politicos are now uncertain as to how they can go on. The question is raised whether Christian faith might still have something to contribute, whether in some way the problems of the political are due to its ignoring of the spiritual.

But before this is greeted by a chorus of 'Told you so' from within the institutions, it must be said that the new concern for spirituality is not a return to old patterns or for old reasons. Those who have been politicized have no wish to go back on their experience. Their concern for spirituality is quite different from those whose spirituality never brought them into conflict with the world at all. Indeed the situation recalls the parable of the Prodigal Son. In that parable the Prodigal is no problem. He did not find what he expected when he took to the road, but at least on his return he understands for the first time what he left behind. The problem figure is the older brother who neither understands what has happened, nor comprehends what he apparently possesses. Or if we continue with biblical images, there is a good deal of evidence in the gospels that those who appreciate spiritual matters are not those who have given their lives to spiritual things, but those who have had to fight the world and have been defeated by it. Radical Christians have tried to change the world, and in their exhaustion and defeat look again at spirituality to discover, if possible, how to be better prepared for the fight.

For those who have been through this experience there is no point in returning to a form of faith which neither criticizes the world nor attempts to change it, a faith which is a form of socialization by which Christians become quiescent citizens and dependable workers. There is no point in looking again at a spirituality which is merely the disguised politics of another world. What has been done has not been enough, but at least the attempt was made. What has been said has not been false, though not enough has been said for it to be true.

Unlike the politicos who have no time for religion, unlike the religious who have no time for the political, the new situation requires a personal integration of two traditions. Previously the agenda was the politicizing of the spiritual, and it was not wrong to attempt this. But in face of the

4

hollowness at the centre we must now ask whether there can be a spiritualizing of the political. In our day 'the criticism of earth turns into the criticism of heaven and the criticism of politics into the criticism of theology', and Marx is made to stand on *his* head. For there is nothing more mindless than political struggle about political issues, nothing more tragic than a politico who wins all battles but loses his own soul – no matter what 'soul' might mean.

Previously Christians fled from a distracting spirituality for the sake of their souls. The political struggle was the right struggle and it was carried on as well as it could be. It is precisely when political struggle is carried on most realistically that questions are uncovered which lead beyond the purely political. Distracting spirituality has been left behind, but at the heart of the political there appears the possibility of a new spirituality. If faith is here empirically based, then the criticism of politics leads on to the area which originally led men to speak of spiritual things and to submit to the criticism of the spirit.

Politicos may well regard all this as a reactionary move, a retreat from political struggle, a falling away into old forms of mystification which lead inevitably to the acceptance of the world as it is – or worse, a legitimization of the world in all its institutionalized evil. This is not the intention, and yet there may have to be some separation of radical Christians from their political comrades. At one time it was difficult to see how Christian faith could contribute anything. Perhaps Christians too readily accepted the agenda given by the politicos. They may have let them down by becoming all but indistinguishable from politicos. But this at least is clear, the question about spirituality is not a turning away from the political. The spiritual dimensions are in this world and in the struggle over this world. It is not a loss of faith in the struggle, but an attempt to find real grounds for faith. To ask about the spiritual is not to give up hope, but to find realistic grounds beyond hoping against hope. It is not to give up in time of trouble, but to discover why political struggle is ineffective. It is not a turning away from the struggle in general, but an attempt to identify the heart of the conflict. It is not a defection when difficulties arise, but an attempt to find new resources to overcome the obstacles.

And so the time is ripe to look to our resources, to inherit our tradition, understanding it for the first time. For the only kind of tradition worth inheriting is one which suggests how we might be faithful now, and this is something we have yet to discover. Spiritual dimensions to a 'religious' life is a far cry from the biblical tradition, which is concerned with the spiritual depths to our social and political lives. The old spirituality had nothing to do with the political, and could not contribute to responsibility. Now the new spirituality seems to emerge from the political. In this dialectic we come to appreciate the realism of the spiritual when we have faced the hollowness of the political. The criticism of the spirit falls both on the religious and the political.

Daniel Berrigan
THE MARK OF THE BEAST

What we are living through in the States is so irrational and so incomprehensible to the majority of our people that one constantly has the sense of being in the middle of a nightmare which has no termination and no inner coherence. So I thought, without further ado, I should turn to a nightmare theme – and one could have thought of many in modern literature – but I prefer a nightmare out of the scriptures. I am going to try to suggest some ideas from the book that Catholics call 'Apocalypse', and Protestants 'Book of Revelation'; I guess it amounts to the same thing. I have always thought that this book, that seems occult and difficult, on account of which so much ink has been spilled, had best be taken, not as some sort of arbitrary nightmare but as a coherent one – a nightmare of experience of the community of faith. Or from another point of view, as a kind of codified message – a political message about belief in a bad time – the code of which lay in the hands of believers, so that the oppressors and the masters could not understand, and the believers could, and indeed, must, because that was the only way to pass on a message of being faithful, being politically alive, being compassionate and sensitive, being there, or as we say up-front, at a time when that was costing you something. So evidently, someone named John who was in a position of some leadership in the church, sent a message to the various churches, which could be read and decodified, understood and pondered by the believers, and which remained utterly blank before those who were presumably in charge of their lives and deaths, and exercising that charge with some bloody consequence.

We badly need a revelation in the States, I don't know the situation here; the Apocalypse is upon us, the revelation is not, for the most part. The genius of this message is to combine both elements, to admit that history is apocalyptic, in the sense of both chaos and outcome, but at the same time to offer a clue, which of course is so desperately needed on all sides. I would like to deal with two sections, which I

7

think have enormous meaning for us, and which I hope have for you also. The first has to do with Chapter 13 and the episode of the Beast risen from the sea, and the response of the community to the Beast and his invitation. The second has to do with an earlier passage, though it is by no means earlier in time – the opening of the scroll of history. I won't try to go into any details of reading, but just try to summarize that thirteenth chapter, and then maybe we can get into a discussion about it.

There is a mysterious Beast that rises from the primordial sea, and he is enormously enticing and violent, and the book makes no bones about his impact upon the community at large, including the community of believers – it is utterly devastating. This is a Beast with many heads, and in verse 3, one of his heads seems to have a mortal wound, but the wound was healed and the beholder had followed the Beast with wonder: so we have a kind of anti-god immediately established, or an anti-Christ. Men worshipped the dragon, for he had given his authority to the Beast (remember the dragon had made an earlier appearance), and they worshipped the Beast, so it is not merely a unity of spirit in awe and wonder, it is now an act of worship in a biblical sense. They worshipped the Beast, saying, 'Who is like the Beast?', which again is a very old echo out of scripture; 'Who is like God?', the name of one of the angels, 'and who can fight against him?' so a sense of hopelessness is immediately engendered, a despair before the wonders possible to this Beast, who seems to have surpassed and entirely replaced an earlier god.

And the Beast who was given a mouth, uttering bloody and blasphemous words, and allowed to exercise authority for a period, opened his mouth to utter blasphemies against God, blaspheming his name and his dwelling, that is those who dwell in heaven. It was allowed only to make war upon the saints and to conquer them.

No bones about it, 'to make war and to conquer'.

And authority was given to it over every tribe and people, tongue and nation, and all who dwell on earth shall worship it, everyone whose name is not written before the foundation of the world in the Book of Life in the Lamb that was slain.

So we have a kind of anti-god set up, almost a kind of anti-Trinity, because this speech is followed by another, and the other speech is more strikingly related to a kind of anti-scripture, an anti-worship, anti-belief.

I saw another Beast that rose out of the earth [the first was out of the sea]; it had two horns like a ram, spoke like a dragon, exercised all authority over the first in his presence, and makes the earth and its inhabitants worship the first Beast.

As Christ, in the deepest sense, in the deepest tradition, leads us to the Father, so this Beast leads us to another. It

> makes the earth and its inhabitants worship the first beast, whose mortal wound has healed. It works great signs, even making fire come down from heaven to earth in the sight of man and by the signs which it is allowed to work in the presence of the Beast deceives those who dwell on earth.

So we have a combination of violence, anti-worship and active deceit. I submit that these are great touchstones to the activity of the state today, in our regard. To sink violence in a kind of religious awe surrounding technological marvels:

> ... bidding them make an image of the Beast which was wounded by the sword, that was allowed to give breath to the image even to speak and cause those who would not worship the image of the Beast to be slain.

I submit that in our country the clue is so evident and so bloody and so immediate as to his activity, that to believer and unbeliever alike, such a book strikes with a force of lightning. The activities of the state, with regard not merely to the people of South East Asia, but to our own people, is a combination of a demand for a religious awe, of deceit and of violence, resulting in this kind of distintegration or consciousness, this breakup of human understanding; the corruption of language and truth; the isolation of good people one from another; the quick tricky formation and breakup of communities almost overnight; the despairing sense on the part of many that they are simply expendable before the Beast, that they are no one, that they are nothing, that both citizenship and faith have been devalued to the point of zero, and that what is actively sought on the part of the state, day after day, year after year, is worship, that is to say, our response to their demand and their claim of ownership, their claim of life and death over us.

I had occasion to say after our trial at Harrisburg, when I was just out of prison last April, that it was quite clear, beyond doubt of any thoughtful person, that we were now as expendable as the Vietnamese, 'we' being defined as any of those who, in the Christian community or elsewhere, should dare to make trouble, in the Vietnamese sense. That is to say, would dare to claim their own soul before the Beast. Well, Chapter 13 becomes even more explicit in this regard.

Also the Beast causes both small and great, both rich and poor, both free and slave [note the enumeration, whereby all are levelled off to the same degree] to be marked on the right hand, or the forehead, so that no one can buy or sell unless he has the mark, that is the name of the Beast or the number of its name. This calls for understanding – let him who has understanding reckon the number of the Beast.

Of course, the mark of the Beast has the most vicious kind of resonance for anyone who has been marked by Christ. I lay the matter out very plainly, because I think the book lays it out very plainly, and I think the state today lays it out very plainly for us. The mark of the Beast is the super-imposition upon the human spirit of the military or para-military claim, which claim designedly erases the claim of Christ, replaces it with a total ethos of violence, a total claim of death whose ruling metaphor is the military kind of defused form. It reaches all across the world, especially across Europe, I would think, laying its claim upon the Third World in the form of life and death control over the religious and economic, social and political life of men and women. So we have, it seems to me, in the latter part of the chapter, a very direct confrontation between the Christian claim and the claims of Caesar, the claim of the state, and both of these are very concrete; and at least some of the experts would say that the mark be placed upon men and women, allowing them to lead the ordinary life of citizens. It is a very worldly thought: the mark allows them to trade, to buy and to sell; without it they simply have no citizenship, they are men and women without a country, without the mark of the Beast.

There is nothing mystical about it all. It is a total claim for numbers, you and myself. The thing is verified in our country obviously through the military induction, but also in a thousand other ways – I don't want to limit it to that. Its most grievous up-front form is the claim over the lives of young people, transforming them from any possibility of (let us call it) a transcendent citizenship, or a breakthrough, or the claim of God on one, transforming them into killers. To be a citizen is to be a killer; it is to wear the mark of the Beast whose first task is *control*, *possession*, and whose methods, as suggested earlier, are that awesome combination of violence, deceit and a kind of pseudo- or quasi-religious awe. 'Who can combat the Beast?' is the great cry that rises from the despairing masses of people, or again, 'Who is like to the Beast?', a direct sentence of worship, twisted around from the Old Testament.

I have a great deal to learn about the thing in England, but it seems to me that in a sense the Vietnamese people and the American people are in a kind of mutual furnace, where the fires of any possible human future are both destroying and creating people. If one were to say that the story of the Vietnamese people could be summed up by the raids of the last two weeks, he would be missing the point, and he would be technologically inexact, let alone spiritually. If any one were to say that the Vietnam war was summing up the American people, he would be just as inexact. If anyone were to say the Vietnam war was summing up the Christian churches in either country, he would be inexact, because the story is not one of total destruction, but it is one of destruction and creation. It is this utter conflict that the book speaks of, gives clues towards; that is to say the call to destroy, or the despair that is to destroy, and then the response. And I have no illusions about that response. The response is quite generally heeded, as the book indeed dolorously predicts. Practically all were found worshipping the Beast – in all the meanings of the horrendous term. But some were not – this is clear in other chapters of the book – and it is made clear in other chapters of our lives; some were not. A very old theology reminds us that the stigma or mark of baptism was taken very seriously in these communities, and that evidently is why the clue about Caesar's claim rests around that metaphor of the mark, now transformed into the mark of the Beast. God, who had totally claimed his community, is now swept aside by Caesar, and the new mark is superimposed, almost like the new brand. As the mark of Christ had claimed one totally for this world and the next, according to certain world vision, a certain code of conduct, a certain attitude let us say towards life and death, so this one. This book, it seems to me, is saying that the very fine equilibrium established in Matthew's gospel where Jesus says 'render to Caesar what is his and to God what is his', that equilibrium is frequently and bloodily upset. As Dorothy Day has said so well, 'the only way to render in a Christian sense to Caesar what is his, is to have very little'. No, the natural impetus, direction and drift of Caesar's power is total. It is this very totalizing of power under the form of total war which the book speaks about.

I would like to suggest that the idea of the total claim leading to total war is not merely an American problem. We just got there first. But we have a lot of friends sort of following on, and reaping where we have sown; dragons' teeth mainly. There is obviously a world drift in our direction, and a great many people, especially in Europe, are anxious that we should do two things. Number one, go ahead of them, because it's a little easier to follow. Number two, succeed in what we set out to do. That's a terrible thing to say. Many people who are not American are very anxious that we should succeed in what we set out to do because their drift, their world vision, is ours. They don't yet have the machinery to put it into motion, but they too want the good life at the expense of the death of others; and when it is laid out, they too are dedicated, in one form or another, more or less, here and there, to the military method of solving human problems, which is to say, the death, the expendability of the innocent, and the helpless and the poor. They themselves, in a manner which is hardly less corrupt than our own, have allowed their religious belief to shift into a gear, a gear which is a killer, a gear which is ideologically rigid, death-ridden and violent. There is no better nation than ours; there are just less developed nations than ours, if you understand me. There is no point in isolating the American example. I speak as one who has suffered within it and know it very well. There is no point in isolating the monstrosity of the super-state. Mr Nixon can leap borders and shake hands with his ideological opposite number and with a kind of mortician's wink at one another, they can understand, whether in China or Russia. He holds your prime minister in thrall in other ways. France is silent. And there are little gasps out of the well-developed small Western nations, but nothing, nothing of indignation at the top, nothing of the sense of the horror of what is being done on people, because, when all is said and done, the ideologies are very much alike. China can mute her claims to purity when the great Westerner hovers in view, and Russia is beyond consideration.

The same view of America, both within and without its borders, would suggest clues to everyone about the general drift of history; about the very approximation – already achieved in Asia – among all kinds of divergent, supposedly warring ideologies, East and West. Deeper than any struggle East and West is now the common acquisitiveness, the commonly accepted violence, the common nuclear stalemate East and West. In that great kind of super-powerful crunch the little nations bleed and die. Which side one is taking can no longer depend upon his status or birth or ideology, or Eastern or Western background. All this has been swept aside by the sinister genius of Mr Nixon and his companions. And what emerges now? In the wisdom of the book, it is this common proffering of the hand or the forehead East and West for the mark of the Beast. And within the great drift towards death, stopping short of the few East and West. This part of the book, then, it seems to me, lays out a powerful and challenging and difficult analysis, without any so-called spiritual solution. Here are the raging historical metaphors into which we are inducted, against which we resist, in virtue of which our imaginations are led captive and enslaved, or which are periodically purified and rejected.

I cannot convey to you, because it would take up much more time than is at our disposal, the way in which the primary, primitive force of those words comes home to any of us that have been through the American courts and have been in the American gaols, and will go on as the international violence is domesticated; as our people slowly, ever so slowly, see their life-images, their hopes, their expectations of one another, diminish; as we see the great cities set themselves up as armed camps; as we see the holy character that should mark human differences and human dealings stiffen into mutual hatred and potential violence; as we see this monstrous deflection away from human needs, or human resources and brains and research and the goods of the earth; as we see the military battle to acclaim the world and community; as we see the Beast claim human life with technology. We see everything of the needs of people, health, education and welfare, declared a kind of issue to one side, the casual issue being the Beast and the feeding of the Beast, and the annual budget.

Mr Nixon declared that health, education and welfare would be severely controlled for the future, but of course there could be no military cuts because of defence needs after Vietnam, that is to say the commitment to feed the Beast. I don't want to dwell indefinitely on our scene, because I think that the resonances around your scene are important. Borders between cultures tend to resolve themselves, to dissolve in the face of the 'facts of life' as the politicians have been talking about. That is to say, when the crunch is on, we are all one. There's a very deep spiritual truth to all this, it seems to me also, and if we accept the fact that the Book of Revelation is trans-historical, that is to say that it is tossed in our direction as well, then we admit that borders of time as well as geographical borders dissolve, and we see the astonishing truth of the march of the Beast through our history and our culture.

In conclusion, I would suggest some concrete points that might be of help in your discussion and workshop groups. The implications for Christians of the Book of the Apocalypse have to do with a style which is in active conflict with what we might call a historical beast. From a Christian point of view, that response might be called many things – in the States the word 'resistance' is quite popular, and it gets across Christian or secular difficulties. In any case it seems to me remarkable that scripture says the battle is joined. In different cultures, according as one lies in the heart of the vortex or at a little bit of distance from it, the style takes on all kinds of different understandings, all kinds of different connotations. I am sure the grievous choices of resistance which we are undergoing have not yet at present reached here. That is not to say that the state is not making similar claims on you; it is to say merely that the state has not pushed so far and so fast. Most of us have felt for long periods of our lives that we could not, indeed did not want to, try to find out if there was a resisting Christian style which was politically relevant and had some roots. Because most of us had been brought up in a watered-down, atrociously deformed Christianity, in which the real biblical message was forbidden us by our teachers and our parents. it was too much to bear with, it was too hard to take. So the idea that the Christian is not a somnolent member in a constant kind of luke-warm acquiescence with the state – this was a very new idea – in fact it was interesting that the state itself had to push us into this kind of understanding because the church had not.

The idea in the United States that there had been a historical conflict between state and church was obscured to us for some two hundred years. Catholics always thought that the main task was to pass from emigrant status and get on the escalator – while the Protestants were way up further; indeed, they were running it, and at some point they would admit us. And so we did. Then suddenly both of us found that there was something wrong with the gears, and that anyone who wanted to climb had better walk. But I wanted to stay with that point because I feel it is one way to clinch the very profound difficulty, indeed the question of our days together. Is it possible that in our communities and in the depths of our souls we admit that resistance is the start-off of Christian life in the world, and if so, what does that mean? Maybe that's a little bit too blown up a plan – maybe that's a little bit too big a plan, but it does issue in this thought, along with the resonances from the other books of the same generation which are almost the same, which speak quite matter-of-factly of people in gaol, people in trouble, people refusing tribute to Caesar in one form or another; people refusing military service and paying for that, and especially that depth of understanding which comes out of the imagination and concrete metaphors which simply says 'the issue is joined'.

Sometimes we suffer from too much history, too much theology and too many teachers, and to get back to scripture can be such a great relief in this regard. Is it possible to admit at this stage of our lives, of our history and our experience – including, that is to say the world, including the Vietnamese people, including South Africa, including Brazil, including Mozambique, and that Third World and the Fourth World, and all the other worlds – is it too much to admit the metaphors of the Book of Revelation, that there is an omniverous Beast, whose ordinary form is the state, which (when the church is most itself) demands of the church as of an opposite respected number, a conflict? So that religion seen by the Beast is no mere resource for the Beast's progress, but a respected opponent, and if so, what form does the response take – which is an extraordinarily difficult question.

Let me say only in conclusion that our experience is that, even for those who in the past few years on occasions of bloody and senseless wars, even for those Christians who have *understood*, in the biblical sense, it has been extraordinarily difficult to create alternatives to the Beast, alternative methods, an alternative faith, an alternative mystique, an alternative world view, and that many who began it so well and with clarity and passion and with what we might call a true sense of things, have ended up mirroring the Beast – have ended up themselves in violence or deceit or rendering religious awe. So the struggle goes on, not merely to confront the Beast, but to create something different, authentic and historical. And that of course brings up the general question of non-violence and its forms and its communities and its methods and its resources and its connection with tradition, and attitude towards prayer and faith and mystery and scripture and all those inspired facts and realities out of which many Christians pretend to walk in the name of something else. In our country they have walked straight towards the Beast, and what the Beast has seen is another Beast. So the question of alternatives.

Colin Winter
NEW COMMUNITIES OF THE SPIRIT

I've a situation to describe which is really impossible, for the person talking to you is a person who is experiencing torture, and yet I've a tremendous yearning to communicate the experiences and the struggle and the courage of my people. And I don't say this in a paternalistic sense, for I speak as an African. I speak as a man who has lost nation and culture and background, and I speak in pride of 'my people'. And before we start we've one of them here, a man who is a living martyr, a witness for the faith in Jesus, who has faced imprisonment for celebrating Holy Communion; who has visited tortured priests in jail, and I don't think we could do any better than to start on a note of glory. *Tate kulu*,* would you stand. Would you welcome him in the name of Christ, Archdeacon Lazarus Haukongo. He comes from a poor church and a martyred church. He comes from a church which I would like to describe to you now, because I have been asked to talk about 'New Communities in the Spirit'.

Let's start with the community Luke describes, the first community, the prototype, the community that every church ought to be. There it is in Acts 2, reading from verse 44.

> And all who believed were together [there was no apartheid]. They had all things in common [they shared, there was no capitalism], and they shared their possessions and their goods and distributed them all, to as many as had need. And day by day attending the Temple together and breaking bread in their homes, they partook of food with glad and generous hearts.

That's the community of the Spirit, the sharing, the caring, the loving, the worshipping, the community of God's Holy Spirit, and this is they of whom I must speak to you. But I come today, not in a judgmental sense. I don't come to lecture you, 'That's it, we've seen it, we've got it! . . . England stinks'. You may think it does, but it is not for me to

* Venerable father.

16

tell you that; that must be your judgment, not mine on you. I come in a spirit of hope, for though we have been tortured and though we have died, and though I can truly say with Paul that I 'bear in my body the marks of the Lord Jesus', yet I come looking for dialogue, for your contribution to my work, and I don't mean as an Anglican.

I want to say that I come with a spirit of hope, because crucifixion is what Jesus calls us to. In the word of Dietrich Bonhoeffer, 'When Jesus calls a man he bids him come and die.' That is what we are training people for in baptism and confirmation. When you say you've come to this conference, what have you come to do? You've come surely to learn how to die, and the best way you can know a man is to ask him, 'What things are you prepared to die for?' And the best way of finding out about your faith and Christianity, about you, is to put it on the line, 'What am I prepared to die for?' I came because I know that there is, in the words of Helder Camara, a 'spirit of idealism'. I thank God for that. You wouldn't have come were that not so. There may be a spirit of cynicism born out of reality, the war in Vietnam, the agonies of Northern Ireland, the ghastly shocking sell-out to commercialism, the exploitation and the grinding down of the poor, the unemployment rate of our country – higher than ever before – and galloping racism everywhere. Yes, we are in one hell of a state, but Jesus reigns and therefore we have hope. One of my priests, who is in Namibia now, describes the battle we are facing as a massive game of chess, in which God and Jesus are arraigned against the forces of evil. God has already got it at checkmate, and you are absolutely tearing yourself around those who are opposed to the spirit of his teaching. You are wriggling, you are squirming, and you think that the power reigns; it doesn't, it's a big lie. That the bloated capitalist and the cruel people and those who torture and those who oppress and those who hold people back, these are not winning. There is a life-surge which is the surge of the Holy Spirit, the Spirit which moves, which lifts us, which moves as he wishes to; this is there. And so I talk to you, not in a spirit of defeatism. I speak to you, not in the spirit of someone who is lost or has been broken, but I speak in the utmost confidence that Jesus reigns and the victory is ours. And I speak conscious, too, that you will contribute to me. Now to the new movements of the Holy Spirit.

First of all, those who asked me to speak had in mind the movement of the Spirit in the Community of Simon the Zealot. I do not want to start there, but with the Africans, for in our white arrogance we tend to think that the only movements which are taking place are white inspired, white intellectual, white liberal. Let's put the picture right. People have been yearning for freedom and for independence in my countries since 1340, since the first white entered the country. They have been dying, they have been imprisoned, and have been tortured. In the Herero war in which the Germans fought, eighty-five thousand blacks went into that war because a terrible act of violence had been perpetrated against them. A Herero prince had married a princess and was making a royal procession of honour coming back through the country with his bride. He saw a German storm-trooper on foot and gave him a lift in his ox-cart, for he was hot and thirsty, tired and hungry. So they moved over and took him in. (Africans know how to share; to learn what the standard of generosity is, live in an African village. We don't need to have old people's homes in my diocese, or orphanages either. Somebody dies . . . they take him in. An old lady with leprosy: 'Come and confirm her, bishop, God has given me a new mother.' 'You'll never find such faith, no, not even in Israel.') And so they gave this man a lift. They went along; night came; lust woke in his body and he tried to violate the newly-wed African princess. Now notice that it was a sexual assault; the man was looking at a lesser breed, as he thought, yet her morality was far higher than this man's, who had been baptized into the name of Christ. She resisted; she wouldn't even agree, and he took out a pistol as she ran to hide in the desert and shot her to pieces. That was the final thing that did it. The Hereros rose, and the great onslaught of German might, which was later to be faced by Britain and other people in the 1914–18 war, was laid against them. This war was a war of total genocide. I asked a German about it in Simonstown, and said: 'Eighty-five thousand people went into that war and only twelve came out, why did you have to destroy so many?' And he rubbed the sabre mark on his face – he was a U-boat commander who had been brought into South Africa now to build up our submarine warfare there. Rubbing it reflectively, he said, 'Ah ha, when we Germans do a job we do it thoroughly.' I said, 'God forgive you for the job you did against the Hereros.' And so they posted their soldiers on the sands of the Kalahari desert, by the waterholes, and as the Hereros came, having been broken in battle, they were forced back to die of thirst in the Kalahari sands. And the church had a part in it, too. Oh yes, our hands are red in blood. The church in Otjimbingue gathered the Hereros together, 'Come to service', the bells rang, and they came and noted there were about fifteen or twenty priests in dark black preaching robes standing around. Then they locked the doors and mowed them down with machine guns. Of course, the missionaries have made a thousand mistakes; the extraordinary thing is love of the African and the love of Christ is so patient with them in our arrogance. You can translate a little bit the first chapter of Genesis when you see a missionary meeting the African people. 'You are naked.' 'I'm naked.' 'Yes you are naked, and that is a sin.' Or, 'Who told you that you are naked?' 'The missionary whom you sent to be with me, he told me I am naked.' 'So cover up your beautiful body.' And we cover it up now from the tip of our chin to the very sole of our feet because Germans are a thorough people – we are now totally covered. And this was the sense of guilt that we brought, a thousand things, but in their love and in their forgiveness, the Africans put up with these things.

So there is this, the violence of the white man in the country; and then, as the nation changes hands in 1919, a glimmer of hope comes in, hope springs eternal, and the people think at last, 'England will take care of us'. Not a bit. Pushed into South Africa and then into the dreaded, hated reserves – and to go into those reserves is to experience a desolation, a Siberia of sand and loneliness – a country, a nation being held back. The very things that you and I take for granted, totally denied to the black. You're educated, you've got a chance at university, at college, a chance to teach. Ask the archdeacon how old he was before he could learn to read and write. I'll tell you, he was twenty, and it was only because a missionary saw him, a heart melted, he walked in miles to get an education. We've men aged forty-seven who will sit down humbly with kids of eleven to learn to read and write. We've boys who face torture, walk out on the Kalahari desert in order to get United Nations scholarships. And South Africa has had my country in her grip for fifty years. Where are our doctors? Where are our scholarly people? Where are our engineers?

I've a quotation here from Herman Toivo. His mother is now in Ondangua. He is suffering life imprisonment on Robben Island. This is his mandate to the South African government when he was brought out for trial for believing in the Declaration of Human Rights. This is what he wrote.

Your government, my lords, undertook a very special responsibility when it was awarded the mandate over us after the First World War. It assumed a sacred trust, to guide us towards independence and to prepare us to take our place among the nations of the world. South Africa has abused that trust because of its belief in racial supremacy and apartheid. We believe that for fifty years South Africa has failed to promote the development of our people. Where are our trained men? The wealth of our country has been used to train your people for leadership and the sacred duty of preparing the indigenous people to take their place among the nations of the world has been ignored.

That is in the words of an African. There is a fellowship of the Holy

Spirit in Robben Island, and I do believe that this fellowship is compounded of suffering. Therefore I do not want us to have an academic interest in all this, a judgmental interest in all this, an interest which may force from the light some lesser verminous breed, and at the same time and in the same process push you out in a spirit of pride and self-contentment. God only knows England is a genius at doing this. And now of course we can't do it so well, can we, because we are rejecting Christ in our own brother, in the Pakistanis and the Indians and blacks in our midst. And yet there is a fellowship of the Holy Spirit on Robben Island. I must tell you about that first.

These are letters smuggled out from this dreaded island off the coast of Cape Town where the leaders and the political prisoners of Namibia are with other freedom fighters. I believe over four thousand political prisoners are now in South Africa.

One of us had his leg amputated after he was assaulted by a member of the South African security forces during his arrest. He was not treated, but was told that he would be treated after his trial. When he arrived here he was not given proper medical treatment. In September 1968 while working at a lime quarry he injured his already injured knee. It swelled out of all proportion. Despite his pain and injury he was forced to go to work and was not treated until he was taken to hospital the next month when his leg was amputated. We complained about it, we complained to the Red Cross representative from Geneva. Nothing was done. Some of us who are suffering from various diseases were told by the doctor that he was aware of their sickness and can do nothing about it to alleviate their suffering. Some of us were even chased away. Do you remember the passage from the Epistle to the Hebrews, 'We were hunted, we went into the caves of the earth and were treated like sheep to the slaughter'?

There it is, this is truly the fellowship of the Holy Spirit. And why? Because they are prepared to die for their freedom. An extraordinary thing to me, and I speak very much as a white person, is the incredible patience of the black man. Now don't use this as a weapon against me, because I've to speak the truth as I see it, and I'm not trying to make a political reason for or against freedom fighters, for or against government, but I want to tell you the truth as I see it. One of the greatest memories for me will be the moment that I went to see, in pilgrimage, the great chief of the Herero people, whose bust stands next to Eleanor Roosevelt on the threshold of the United Nations. What a vision, what a possibility is there, and yet still being brought to naught by the machinations of the Western world is this man's original petition since 1946. The Third World knocking for justice, for freedom, for all the very things we are supposed to believe in, and yet we are still turning them away empty. After listening to Chief Hosea Kutako describing his youth, I asked him then, 'And what of the future?' 'You know we want a Namibia, South West Africa, free to welcome and to use the gifts and talents of all its people. We do not want to send the white man away. You see, bishop, we don't hate the white man, we need the white man.' What was he speaking of? He wasn't speaking as of some sort of black who felt inferior to the white. He was speaking of a state which was going to use the services and the ability, the God-given gifts of every single person of that community. This is what the Namibia, the freedom fighters and the people within the black community want. They're sick to death of racism. Here are the words of Nelson Mandela.

During my lifetime I dedicated myself to this struggle of the African people. I have fought against white domination and I have fought against black domination. I have cherished the idea of a democratic and free society in which all people live together in harmony with equal opportunity. It is an ideal which I hope to live for and achieve, but if need be it is an ideal for which I am prepared to die.

So will you please take that and enshrine it in your hearts. That this is the society that we yearn for, which will one day be achieved, yes, through suffering, because we believe that it is the society that God wants in South Africa.

The Communities of the Holy Spirit. You have to come with me in your imagination to the mines of my country. Come knowing that the white man is there to rip off the vast resources from Namibia and to use it in America, in the American Metal Climax Company, in Rio Tinto, to prop up the standard of living in America and Britain. Our country has been called 'the most exploited country in history', because thirty per cent of the gross national product is removed from it. People in the United States and elsewhere are receiving thirty per cent return on investment from certain mines in my country, and the African as little as fifteen shillings per week. No chance to have your wife or your child with you, but you are brought, and in the words of a Swapo leader who has now been put under a banishment order, 'You are sold like a petrol drum or like a goat in my country'. Come to those little communities then and what will you find? Communities of the Holy Spirit, people cannot read or write, the only book they have is either a New Testament or a catechism, or a tiny little hymnal, and the man who may have had only one year of formal education teaching other people to read and write, and doing it with such graciousness that your heart would melt. Come out with Stephen Hayes in a Land Rover in response to a letter which I have received printed in great capital letters. 'My bishop, we greet you in the name of the King of Kings world over. May the light of Christ shine upon you and upon all our white brothers. Bishop, please send us books. We want catechisms and standard two books, and when you come, bishop, please come prepared to baptize and confirm some of the brethren.' And this is it. A man who is just there, a miner who is doing the work of an apostle of Jesus Christ. And so you come, but first of all they will not give you a permit, and secondly you've to break the law to get in, but you get in. And then a white man bursts in who has been to church every Sunday. What God is he worshipping, that he rejects him day by day in his fellows around him? He grabs all the literature and says to Stephen Hayes, 'These are communist Bibles.' I did three years in theology at Oxford, but I had no answer for the man when he said that. My professors had never told me how to lecture a congenital idiot.

Wherever you move you see these gatherings of the Holy Spirit, and I've never seen anything more beautiful in my life. Fr George Pearce, a great evangelist from America, who is now working with the Dakota Indians, used to take a Land Rover and minister across my diocese of 318,000 square miles. One time we found a little clump of men washing themselves as the sun was setting over the sands of the Kalahari desert, and as we drove up, these men who have not seen their wives and their children for eighteen months, men who have a brass ring around their arms – the shackles of the contract labour system – these men came running, dropping shovels and spades and God knows what else. 'Here's our priest, here is our brothers,' and gathering around, a service would take place (segregated from the lonely white man fifty yards up the road) with that gorgeous evening hymn which was sung in the light of the lamps of the Temple, 'Hail, gladdening light, of his pure glory poured'. Listen to those voices raise it up to heaven as the evening office of the church takes place and realize what the Spirit of Jesus means: those who share with each other and those whose spirits speak with each other and bind people together in such lonely places.

And now finally I am ready to tell you about the other community, the community of Simon the Zealot.

I suppose every man has a dream. I had a dream when I went to South Africa and the dream often became a nightmare, because I was foolish enough to believe that wherever Christians met they would be able to see Christ in other people, because that was what it was all about. At least, I thought so. I thought every church was composed of people who believed it. Then like a child who one day believes that the world is beautiful and somebody tells him a filthy way of describing sex, dirty and vile and horrid – and it isn't at all, because it's the most beautiful act that one human being can administer to another, the sacramental act of love, where two people become one, one flesh – and the shock nearly kills you when you see it. Then you realize that you cannot destroy this, that you can't force racism out of a man by a gun, by hate, or by battling with him or by banishing him, or by passing laws and rules because, beloved, we are not under the law, we are under the Spirit of Jesus; and you can't do it by guns and tanks, because this nation took on the whole British nation in the Anglo-Boer War and beat her, so you can't do it by that. Then how will you do it? I'm not absolutely sure that I know, but I know his method and I know his way and I take it in all humility, the way through suffering and martyrdom.

So I've seen once in a little vision the way the church could be in France. Missionary priests who opened up their very doors to the very pagans. 'Little brothers of the country' they were called. Men who spoke the same accent as the people. These were no Oxford or Cambridge Joes who couldn't even relate at all except intellectually, to the agonies and the problems of their flock, but men who were bone of their bone, hewn out of the very rock of the people among whom they worked. We came then to see this and to plant it in Namibia. I had a dream, a dream of 'a remnant'. Not a remnant that was going to be like the Pharisees, withdrawn, but a remnant where blacks could come and see the very body of Christ. Because, when I became dean of the cathedral, I stood with a black in the street and spoke to him and said, 'What is that building over there?' He replied and said, 'It's a white church, baas*.' I said, in agony, 'Why do you call me baas?' 'Because you are white.' 'And what do you call your priests in Ovamboland?' A smile, a radiant smile, 'Oh, there we call them father.' One family, and this was the beginning of it. The whites frightened to death. It's easy to be judgmental about white people in South Africa. Would you give up your job because of your belief? Would you face the police for going to church on Sunday morning? If after the service the secret police came in and said, 'What did the bishop say? You know he's a communist.' When your mother comes to you, worst of all and says, 'Look, I've inched and pinched to get you to university. Don't go any more to that meeting for God's sake, for love of me.' James Joyce faced it with his mother, you remember? 'Say a prayer for me, son, I'm

* Master.

23

dying.' He was too honest; but how many people have the integrity of Joyce? So try to get the balance and there it is. We had a vision. 'Of course we've integrated the cathedral,' we said, 'of course these are your brothers and sisters in Jesus; of course we've a black priest on the staff of the cathedral . . .' But does that make it Christian? Does that make Holy Communion holy? Not a bit. And when you go out into the parish and the people are standing in little blobs of black and white, the blacks in the corner, the whites over there, what have you achieved? And so, you see, it had to be done through the fellowship of the Holy Spirit, and we had to say, 'Look, this is the way; walk in it.' So God formed the community of Simon the Zealot.

Someone described it as a desert flower that comes up terribly beautiful and terribly fragile and then it dies. I don't believe it has died. Let me describe to you some of the people, let me tell you what they were doing. David de Beer came up from John Davis' university, the University of Witwatersrand. He wanted to do something positive to get rid of guilt. He wanted to have the right to love people just as people. He wanted to work as a hospital secretary and auditor in Ovamboland, in a hospital. He lasted just a week. He was deported. shut out, and so we grabbed him. He gave me an opportunity to have an episcopate which was really something that I believe ought to have been. Not a bishop behind a desk, not a bishop protected by archdeacons and a hierarchy, but a bishop who would say, 'Keep that door open and if any black comes in he's Jesus. Let him come straight in and see me, and if we've got this meeting or that meeting on, it's stopped, for this man has walked twenty or thirty miles to see me.' And this is what happened in the Community of the Holy Spirit, where people mattered more than money, and statistics, and God knows what else.

Stephen Hayes, what a guy! He looks like Castro with a biretta on! Asked to do duty in a church in South Africa, a white middle-class ultra, the equivalent of a high Anglican church in Bognor Regis. He only got to do two Sundays there. He said to them, 'We're going to sing songs like in England, "Lord of the Dance" and "Oh Freedom" and things like this.' So the churchwardens started looking askance, and they were talking to each other at the back. In the middle he said, 'If anyone wants to dance get up and dance.' And he brought some African people in who loved dancing, and they danced; and he was unfrocked. One service, that was all it took – OUT! The church has a certain Germanic efficiency when it's dealing with important things like that. You can't profane it. You see, kids, dancing is filthy, and so they had him out. I heard about it and I wrote a letter saying 'I've nothing to offer you; I can't pay you, but come out.' And he came and he arrived. What a man! A man whose job was just to see the Africans and to relate to them. To be the servant of the people, the voice of the people.

And then another guy, fantastic, whom God calls. Somebody who was a big-time lawyer, had great ambitions and was a brilliant cricketer. He came with his wife. Her job was to go into the highways and the byways. If I say the words to you now, 'Old People's Home', what comes into mind? Come into the old people's home in Katutura. See where the water is, it's a toilet pan, that's broken and people wash in it and urinate in it. Come and see the places they are living in, sacks pushed into a corner. Come and see the food; it's like the food that was given to concentration camp victims. And they are nobody's responsibility. The whites in England are no worse and no better than the whites here. No worse and no better, because old people die in England in similar circumstances. You've seen it. What has gone wrong? There is absolutely no one listening, no contact at all between you and that suffering group of people. And one of the worst experiences of my life was when Friday after Friday I used to go in with forty gallons of soup and milk and know it was not enough, and stand there giving it out watching nervously as the queue got bigger and bigger. So at the end I was just giving a piece of biscuit *that* size. And then the nobility of the people as they would come and thank me for nothing. 'Thank you bishop for coming . . . We know that the bishop cares about us.' And they went away empty. Jill Nicholson was in there. Arthur Dibble's wife had died of cancer. 'Whom God sends. The Spirit of God moves, the wind blows and unknown people answer.' His wife had died of cancer, he was going through deep depression, and so he came out to give us a year or two. He came out, and I can hear him pray as the community met in our tiny little cathedral, day after day to break bread . . . I hear Arthur Dibble speak about his wife who was 'with Jesus in the presence of the radiance of your glory'. This told me what the communion of saints was all about. I saw it in his face as he prayed.

And of course the black – the guy who swept the office floor and came into our conference at Windhoek. We discovered he was an evangelist. Keep Billy Graham! Billy Graham is way back as far as our country is concerned. This guy was in the compound every day selling them New Testaments. Six thousand men. Sodomy, every type of vice you could think of was there, 'but in all their afflictions he was afflicted'.

Then Richard Wood. He had married an Afrikaaner, and hitch-hiked up. He wanted to find a Franciscan way of life and he came to us. I'm telling you that it would be an impossible thing to describe. How do you describe love? Tell me how you do define it. But you've seen it, and it's a very beautiful experience. How do you define suffering;

when people reject you because you've become black by identification? So Dave de Beer moves into the camps and calls me to a confirmation. Have you ever confirmed drunken people? I have. You go in and the people are so alone, so rejected that they feel vile, and the only way out is the bottle. Have you ever seen people who are so totally indoctrinated that they no longer believe that they are anybody, they're just dirt, and so they live according to that model and that image? And there the great campaign began because we believe the whole thing is that you have to overcome evil with good. Does that sound arrogant? Don't ask us what our policy was; don't ask us what our theology was; we just wanted to love people and we just wanted to be there, whatever we could do to help, to assist. We wanted to listen to them, and I think we were rewarded in the process. So we produced a thing called 'News of the World'. Can you believe it? There's an irony there. Not the sort of dirt that was churned out week after week in this country, but dirt of a different hue. The fact that Chief Clemens Kapuuo now had a voice for his Herero people. The fact that when the men from the Kaokoveld came down we were able to say to them, 'What do you want us to do?' asking in terms of church or schools or bread. 'What do you want for the Kaokoveld?' 'Freedom.' And it went in; the power of the written word. We were there to get underneath a nation in its struggle, to become the voice of the oppressed. But let's just finish by saying a few extra words about them.

Radio, television, we tried to face the whole lot. We said that the job of the bishop is not to protect the church, that's God's job; the job of a bishop is to speak the truth in love and this we tried to do. And I don't think we failed. And if you ask me if we're broken-hearted, of course we are. If you love somebody dearly . . . Speak to a man who is divorced and ask him if he is proud of it. Ask him if he would go back tomorrow. Of course he would. But the great situation was that in all this the blacks realized that they could see a community of God's Holy Spirit, and you see there would be no church left – no church as we know it, unless this had been so. There are over one thousand breakaway churches in Johannesburg, a thousand groups of people who have said 'No' to the white man's God. And can you blame them? You would be proud of them if you were there. We were not doing it to protect the unity of the church, we were doing it because we believed this was the way. Sermons were preached, of course; the whites moved away from us, of course; paid informers ratted on us, of course. I can't describe too much of the suffering, I think I'd cry if I did. And there was the greatest event that has happened, a prophetic event, an event that will go down in history, in the liberation movement in their finest hour, the Ovambo strike. Where thirteen thousand men said 'No' to Vorster. Vorster, who has lied and cheated. Vorster, who at the United Nations has said that the African is quite content with the contract labour system and that the Bantustans are the only way to keep order. And then twelve men brought to prison in manacles for being the strike leaders. One of them kept a strike diary and I quote from it.

And you can see that this strike was, in the words of Bishop Mize, 'the work of the Holy Spirit'. 'Love thy neighbour as thyself,' says the commandment of God. We don't want the contract labour system any more because we have no human rights. It denies us recognition as human beings. Due to the contract the Ovambos are not regarded as people. The word of God says that Christ died to free people. The Ovambo are not free of the contract.

There we have it, a manifesto for the whole of Southern Africa. 'We don't believe in a system which sells people,' and the church took its stand and we raised two hundred pounds a day to defend them. We were the only ones in court on the white side; the black side, of course, was packed. No other church leaders, no other people of standing were there, just the Community of Simon the Zealot, the community of God's Holy Spirit.

But then we are deported; have we lost? No, for we believe the liberation movement now is with the Africans and we believe they have the power and the ability to do it. And I believe that you too can help in this struggle, by your knowledge, by information, by eradicating racism out of Britain, by making Britain have a conscience again and a morality again. You speak of 'permissiveness'. What do you mean? Do we mean the people who are receiving massive returns on investments in Rio Tinto? Do you mean the people who are living in fabulous homes, who are taking in the sweated products of these people in the mines? Of course you do – and that's the permissiveness I speak of.

But I think of David de Beer now under a banning order, and Stephen Hayes and the other people, deported from Damaraland. The movement still goes on. You can't quench the Holy Spirit. So I finish, not in a blaze of glory, but with a great deal of suffering, with a feeling of pride, too, and humility at what God has done. How has he done it? Not through giants, certainly. Not through intellectual men. In the last quotation, this is how I see them, will always see them. Paul, to the people of Corinth.

Consider your calling brethren. Not many of you are wise according to worldly semblance. Not many of you are of noble birth, but God chose what is foolish in the world to shame the wise. God chose what is weak in the world to shame the strong. God chose what is low and despised in the world, even things that are not, to bring to naught things that are so, that no human being might boast in the presence of God. And he is the source of your life in Christ Jesus whom God made our wisdom our sanctification and our redemption. Therefore it is written, 'Let him who boasts, boast of the Lord'.

There it is, the best I can do. Love and peace be with you all.

Jim Forest
COMMUNITIES OF RESISTANCE

Before we gather in conversation together perhaps you would be willing to join in a kind of experiment together. The experiment is a very simple one. It's an experiment which has been given to us – or renewed for us – by various traditions, by the traditions of Buddhism, Judaism, Christianity and even Marxism. It is also for people who choose not to have traditions, or at least try not to have traditions. It is the tradition, a non-tradition of silence, rooted in our knowing or intuiting that there are times for silence. Perhaps this could be a time for silence or for some approximation of silence. Not a silence, however, that tapes closed anyone's mouth. There are times – as Quakers have shown – when in fact silence invites us to speak words that describe the soul of the silence. So it's a very simple thing. Let us try it, though it may prove to work very *badly* amongst us, coming as we do from so many points of view and so many ways of living and seeing and hearing and of speaking. Let us take the risk of silence even as we recall that there is a radio station in New York that fires its announcers if they allow five seconds of silence to go out on the air. Perhaps all of us would risk being fired by that radio station this morning.

There followed a ten-minute silence at the end of which Jim and Dan stood up and distributed loaves of bread among the people present as Dan spoke the following words:

As in the communities where we come from, there are those upon whom the bombs are falling and those who are in camps or prisons and hospitals and are separated from their families and those they love, not by choice but by the iron will of war. Remembering them, we bless this bread and we eat this bread as the hope of men and women, that all may be fed.

I sometimes describe myself as a fallen-away journalist, but I don't think that is really true. Although I no longer work for newspapers I have *become* a kind of walking newspaper, and part of my life, unless in prison, is walking and travelling around and bringing bits of news. Some of it is not so cheerful, and some of it absolutely, transcendingly ecstatic – about things that I know are happening and people that I know who are alive. 'People who are alive'; I don't think it's possible to talk about 'being alive' until we are willing to deal with the possibility that we are not seeing the death, or knowing the death, or smelling the death or tasting the death that is the familiar experience of life for so many of our relatives in the family of life. To get at this, let me tell you a little story, a true story that has haunted me for years.

There was a woman, a young woman named Kitty Genovese who lived in New York city in an area called Kew Gardens. She worked as a secretary in some gigantic insurance company with its four-hundred storey buildings with three thousand miles of air conditioning and glass and aluminium and neon lights. She came home on the subway or the bus every night, experiencing that horrendous and humiliating pilgrimage that millions of people in all parts of the urban world are forced to make twice a day in order to survive and provide for their families.

She got off the bus that night and began walking the quarter mile to her apartment building. Now on one side of the street there are some of those 1930–1940 apartment buildings (that's old in America), and on the other side there was the park. She walked on the park side. There was some poor deranged figure hiding in the bushes there and he came out with a knife and he stabbed her as she walked by in the dark, and she fell to the pavement. She was only slightly injured. The coroner thought that the first stab was in the lower part of her back and did not touch any important organs. It hurt a great deal and made it impossible to walk because the pain was so proximate to her spine. She cried out for help. The man was terrified and ran back into the park. Across the street, in the four-storey apartment building, people heard her cries. In fact forty families later admitted that they had heard her cries. A few venetian blinds tipped open, a few went up. A couple of windows were opened, some lights went on. People looked out from their windows and they saw Kitty Genovese there on the street. They saw the small pool of blood on the pavement. They looked, and then the venetian blinds tipped closed again. Perhaps one or two, though they did not admit it, stayed and watched for a while as if it were television without commercials, as you have here in this country. The knife and its man came back out from the bushes again, because he discovered nobody had come. He stabbed Kitty Genovese again and again. Again she cried out for help and again there was a flicker of interest in the apartment building across the street. But again nobody came. Finally Kitty Genovese was dead.

No one called the police. No one opened their window and screamed out. No one left their apartment and went down to the street to drag her to safety or try to frighten away this man. She died. And according to the Police Commissioner in New York, her death and its circumstances were not at all newsworthy. The police department didn't put out a press release or have news conferences. But it happened that the *New York Times* had just appointed a new city editor, a man named Rosenthal, and as it was his job during his first few weeks to have lunch with city officials, he happened to have lunch with the Police Commissioner of New York the day after Kitty Genovese's death. The Police Commissioner mentioned that one of the police department's main problems was that nobody so much as calls the police even when murder is occurring. 'I'll give you an example,' he said, telling Rosenthal about Kitty's murder. Rosenthal, fresh to his job, decided it was 'news'. And so the story made its way into the world's crowded ear.

To me it became a kind of microcosm of the entire culture which I know and have grown up in and have been a part of. Now it may be that there are few people here who would have acted in that situation like any of the witnesses in Kew Gardens. I am not saying that we would all have failed to use the telephone, failed to have called out, failed to have intervened. I pray that we are capable of that here, that we have got to that point – and perhaps even beyond that point. But we live in a world in which our windows are open, not just to the park across the street, but to Vietnam and Northern Ireland, to South Africa, to Mozambique, to the Philippines, to Harlem and to Angola. We can see where we wish to see. Technology at last has made it possible for our retinas to see nearly as far as we dare. Our windows look out, not only on Kitty Genovese being murdered, but on people in countless numbers being starved to death, being bored to death, being shot and bombed and burned to death, being treated as objects. We see that all the time. And our response is often even less interesting than those forty witnessing families. They at least allowed their eyes to stare at the scene for a little while and God knows what passed through their minds.

Kitty Genovese's death and the forty families who witnessed it describe the twentieth century; our walled-up consciences, our eyes which dare not experience any real communions. Sure, we *look* at it, we cannot avoid looking. We would be ashamed of ourselves if we never looked at the news, never glanced at a newspaper. But that's very much the limit. So today I want to discuss the possibilities of our being the kind of forty-first families that would work very hard to see to it that all the Kitty Genoveses and Thich Nhat Hahns and Cao Ngro Phuongs and all the people of the world might be able to walk home at night without being killed.

I have been a part of several families that have worked at this. People who have consciously attempted a quality of contact with reality that presupposes the willingness to respond. I think for example of the Catholic Worker and the War Resisters' League and the Fellowship of Reconciliation; I think of the resistance communities that we have put together and lived with and gone to prison with and come out of prison with. I think of all the little houses of hospitality scattered around the countryside of America and the cities of America, so often launched by people marked by criminal records, which for us has been a way of being marked by the gospels and marked by the love of bread; we are so marked by these that we sometimes are able to celebrate – despite all the grim news – a mysterious joy. Even though we *know* we are breathing in the ashes of the dead, even though we know lives are still on fire, we are able to imagine responses and able to experience another word for hope. Out of which comes a life in which sacrifice is real, but quite different from masochism.

It is the Catholic Worker I keep thinking of again and again, which has formed and birthed and delivered and pulled us forward again and again and again in the American Community. I have been thinking about that series of little places where people are welcomed without question and where the editors are perennially going to jail, and where we see a great deal of death and of people dying in doorways, where we insist that there is some connection between the people who are dying in the doorways on our streets and the people who are dying in their houses in Indochina. Thinking of the Catholic Worker I think how very simple the whole thing is. How incredibly simple. None of us, for example, has to be an intellectual. I don't have to be an intellectual to respond, to see, to keep the windows open, to be able to run out into the street. It's all in the gospels. Think of Chapter 25 of St Matthew's gospel; 'I was hungry and you fed me, I had no place to stay and you took me in. I was thirsty and you took care of my thirst. I was sick and you nursed me. I was in prison and you came to be with me.' These are the criteria of judgment, these are the criteria of *life* according to him, according to my brother Jesus, and it has marked all of us, Christian and non-Christian, in a very special way before and since. It's the very core of the whole Catholic Worker experience. We are involved in a premeditated attempt to be people of mercy and so a huge range of possibilities are opened up for us, as well as thousands closed. Obviously, for example, pacifism has been absolutely inescapable to us; if we are going to talk about feeding hungry people and being with hungry people, we are certainly not going to be part of any process which creates hungry people. We are certainly not going to be part of any process which strips or burns the clothes or skins from people's backs. We are certainly not going to be part of the process that creates the *need* for hospitality of which war is the most glaring and ultimate example. We are not going to be part of any of these things. These possibilities are forever closed to us. We are not going to *create* the need that we are called to respond to. We are simply going to respond to that need – and thus, at the same moment, to ask questions, not simply about how to respond today to this particular person's problems, but to ask how it is that such a problem exists. We see in that gospel an invitation to ask questions about suffering and especially *unnecessary* suffering, which is what the term 'oppression' really means. How does it happen to be that Kitty Genovese is knocked down and knifed dead, and how is it that no one puts their life in the way of her death?

Inevitably as we explore the works of mercy in our day-to-day contact with people who have been thrust out of society and left to die on the streets, we come to make certain connections. It isn't just our small block. We come to see that people are being thrust out on the streets in huge numbers in other parts of the world – and for essentially the same reasons. You know Daniel Berrigan uses the phrase, 'dread of life'. We can speak of these things in very economic and analytical terms, but it keeps coming back to this deep fear of touching and of being touched, of actually having a moment of hot contact with the reality of another's life; to *taste* another's life, to overcome the fear of that, the fear of the stripping that might happen if I discover that another person has needs. If I really discover the need is there and feel that person's life has been something like my own, I might have to give something up, I might have to break the bread and pass it out instead of keeping it for a hungry day.

Communion – community – communication. It is in the ironic position of attempting to be in communion with people, to feel their lives and urgencies and needs, that we discover the possibility of giving. Giving is a way of life, it's not a voluntary thing, you know. If you've looked out the window and you fail to respond, you're dead. If you want to be alive, it's a necessity to respond. So we look out that window and we see what is happening. We break out of the place. And while responding we discover that, while everybody has assured us that we were going to be dead out there, that life on the other side of the window would be miserable and couldn't possibly be satisfied any more, that our basic needs couldn't be met in that kind of response, we discover instead that for the first time in our lives we are beginning to feel the meaning of the word 'happiness'. We are beginning to understand the gospels. We are beginning to understand why it is that Jesus begins the beatitudes – a meditation on happiness – with a few words on the subject of poverty and moves on. We begin to understand the ironic relationship between the willingness to risk and the possibility of feeling joy, of having joy. As Leon Bloy said, 'The most infallible sign of the presence of God is joy.' We discover for the first time that it is possible to be joyful, just when we are on the way – as others judge – to death. For the gospels are suddenly no longer insane. They make sense, and we discover there are absolutely no ways in which we can close ourselves off from suffering without ourselves being made dead. Such is the insight lived out daily at the Catholic Worker – and out of that, in Chicago and San Francisco and Milwaukee and all these different places has emerged much of what we know of now as The Resistance.

I think, too, of the example of David Miller whose wife and children are here in front of me, who was part of the Catholic Worker in 1965. It was he who lit our consciences on fire by taking his draft card and lighting it on fire in 1965. Do you recall the horror and astonishment of an amazing number of people about that? It surprised us more than any. *We* expected everybody to be too dead by then to notice a burning piece of paper. From that act right out of the Catholic Worker, a community of people emerged who began to see in the institution of conscription the kind of embodiment of our whole way of life; in every turn of life, not only in the military but in school and church, in business and subways, we realized we were objects to be subjected to conscription, to be told *how* to go, *where* to go, *what* to say, *what* to wear, how *not* to talk, what *not* to say, what to be in *dread* of, who to *work* for, *who to be willing to kill*. We saw in conscription what our whole society was about and it was symbolized by a draft card. We went on from there, with Philip Berrigan pouring blood with his friends in Baltimore, not on draft cards but draft records. We went on from there to see the records not just as objects to be stained but objects to be made useless. We began to re-cycle them. We found in these moments we were rediscovering the possibilities of worship, we were finally finding a current way of articulating the gospels and finally finding a way of worship. For while these actions were obviously political, they were even more deeply spiritual, religious, liturgical events. This was the way that we could celebrate and articulate the Mass, the Book, and it was inconceivable for us to speak of either Book or Bread as long as our contact with the draft was a contact of syllables thrown into the air and into other people's ears. It was only when we took this sacred property of the state, pieces of paper, and dared to suggest that this paper was responsible for death, and that this kind of property had no right to exist, that ears opened, that people in their anger, in their puzzlement became capable of wondering about conscience, wondering about life, wondering about the possibility of their lives not being subject to conscription wherever they happen to be.

There is a line in a poem of W. H. Auden's, who is a wonderful traditionalist but with the only kind of tradition worth having. He says, 'Prohibit sharply the rehearsed response.' In our experiments with resistance we were a scandal to pacifists as well as militarists in what we did – and in what we continue to do sometimes. It was not a rehearsed response. It was not something that Gandhi or Martin Luther King or Henry David Thoreau had done. It was even something that was a scandal to some of our friends within the Catholic Worker. Perhaps they thought that the subscription lists would get burnt by some counterpart of ours! A just worry. But we broke out of the rehearsed response in solidarity with a tradition which is only valuable because it is continually proposed that we do just that. The tradition is to invent. We did it in community; we did it with silence; we did it with bread and wine; we did it with Jews. We did it without any money, and we loved it. We were able to breathe, we were able to feel our hearts beating and the sound of ourselves again. We were able to embrace each other in a society that does not particularly like embracing – except vicariously in 'x' rated movies. We did not end the war but we began finding an element of the way out, a way of community, and of resistance and of invention that prays so to multiply that we will at last no longer need to kill, no longer need to keep blind. For all its failure, this was the only kind of success that we could see in our society; the only place where we saw the Bible and did not try to escape the room. It was the only way we could look at each other; the only way we could talk about love.

I wish that we could bring some of our friends here. I wish the Atlantic Ocean were just a river, that we could have rafts, that we could bring you across to see what is going on, just as I wish you could give us some of the things you have learnt in your attempts to create some sanity on this island. Perhaps you have sensed in some of the things that have happened, it's not merely a convention of speeches that we have, it's a way of being together, of trying to see the world; and of trying to invent responses that are new and honest.

As you can see, I am not an orator. As I said in the introduction, I am just a traveller. I would hope that in our conversation this morning we could focus very much on the inside of these experiences and the possibility that the experiences we have been having in our struggle that has been brought on mostly by the war, to establish more of a community across the water may also be useful to yourselves. I hope also that they will allow us to bring back with us some of the things you are doing or would like to do, or think valuable. I think there are really things that bring people together, that a lot of the ideological problems that have been expressed here will find a place within community, so that the community becomes richer for it.

Daniel Berrigan
SANITY IN FACE OF THE BEAST

It has been said very often in my country, to the point where it has become part of our folklore, that the British are a 'laconic tribe'. I want you to know that I will spend the rest of my life countering that calumny. I had come here with the expectation that the meeting would be two part Zen and one part Quaker, but I was very shortly to see about that. Since then I have been almost talked to death, indeed have been listened almost to death. I described yesterday's experience as being 'nibbled to death by ducks', and someone else on the programme said he had been 'stoned to death by marshmallows'. We have both risen temporarily from death this morning, to face you inexorably once more. I am going to be mercifully brief, and we will try to get a discussion going.

The Book of Apocalypse is an extraordinarily worldly book, because it is religious; not in the dessicated sense of calling God dead, by people in pursuit of their own interests in the name of post-religion, but as a very vital and primitive religious document. I think that's clear. God's interest is not in the church as such, but in creation, including the church, and that is what the book is about – the church in a bad society, in a bad time, with the kind of sobering resonance that the time spoken of in the book is bound to be almost usual time. That is a recurrent circumstance, a recurrent confrontation, a recurrent necessity of understanding and of attitude. Therefore in line with our topic, and without trying to force things, it seems to me that the Bible is both spiritual and political in the sense of conveying a vision of humanity, man and woman, concrete and sinful, possibly in death redeemed, but entirely fleshly and *there*, visibly, morally at a crossroad (not in outer space, not in a vacuum, not denuded other than by the bloody necessity of choices day after day, or the unbloody absence of violence both within and without), but there as such, as we ourselves face the experience, within and without, day after day, in our society.

We were talking last time about that very distressing Chapter 13 and the meaning of the Beast. As I had cause to learn since, many in the conference were shaken by that whole concept, were trying to deal with it, and it came again and again, in a lot of ways, as far as I could judge. Remember that the particular episode closes with the idea of a mark, on which I want to dwell very briefly. The Greek for the word is *stigma*, a *stigma* from the Beast, presumably indelible, and again an extraordinarily kind of pedestrian, worldly tactic. People are lined up in queues to be stamped, as kind of human beasts, walking integers, citizens denuded of all spiritual content. That is not a matter of indifference, as we learn in another context in Luke, where Joseph and Mary had to set out for Bethlehem on a kind of parallel border of the state of Caesar to return to their place of birth, there to be stamped – be part of the census. We have that as the normal scene of the world here, and I think it is worth dwelling on because it has such powerful and constant meaning for the citzen who is also a believer. The book says quite openly that without this stamp you cannot live, you cannot live in the state, you cannot do the ordinary stuff like buying and selling. Anyone who finds the stamping of his body objectionable from any point of view – let's say religious, or even human, that one be lined up and marked that way – anyone who kind of bows out of that little programme is in trouble, can't function. You have to show your identity card everywhere, and it can be demanded of you by the police. The Roman thing is a little bit more primitive, a little more frightening, it is done right on the body. In the States you have to have your card with you, and this tends to be true almost everywhere. There are borders all over the place within the States. Some of the experts say that the mark had a very special meaning in Rome, because Rome was always at war. Rome was an imperialist state and it was spreading out in all directions. It needed not only human beings, it needed cannon fodder, it needed soldiers. The real meaning of the census was to tell the emperor to what extent all this was available, where the soldiers were, and where they could be gathered up. So they were numbered, all citizens were numbered so that this could get under way. This common resource of violence would always be available.

This is very interesting because it put the community of believers in an immediate conflict. John ironically uses the same word for this mark as the early Fathers adopted later in talking about baptism. These people had already been marked by the *stigma*, and their community and their sign of belonging was already a matter of fact, on record. They were marked by Christ as belonging to him, and that becomes a great theme. Then Caesar comes and says, 'No, I want to mark you and for a very special reason, for reasons of violence, for reasons which are ultimately those of violence, and also (to locate those things we spoke of earlier), for reasons of deceit and for reasons of religious awe.' The declaration, as the community understood very well, the stigmatizing, the lining up, the stamping, the marking, was in fact a parody of baptism. It therefore involved one immediately in a kind of worldly call to idolatry. 'Line up and adore the beast' (who as we know also, according to the commentary, took the form of the emperor's statue). The Beast was the name that John gave to this enormous statue which Augustus had raised and which we are told was even wired for sound, was a kind of idol. It spoke to the people and amplified and exaggerated the statue of this human being into some demigod, and demanded of them a religious response, that is to say, 'Here are our lives, here we are for death.'

So the crisis I wanted to point out was the ordinary worldly one. It was the practical question 'Can we live in that kind of totalization of the state that demands of us systematic violence, war-making, deception and a deflection of our religious life into the Emperor's uses?' Of course the response had to be 'No, no, this could not be done.' I think that we have often a kind of misty view of these early conflicts. In the world the Christian cannot be conscripted into violence, and that is a kind of parameter of his activity. That is where he really has to stand. How that can be translated into various societies, of course, has to be thought out carefully. How can that reflect itself here? The matter is so much clearer in our country right now and has both advantages and disadvantages. As we have been trying to explore in the workshops, it seems to me that the English and the Irish and the Scots, and anyone else, any other Western nations, cannot get by by reading Revelation as though it were aimed at Americans. The fact is that every state, great or small, I submit, is about as bad as it can be, according to its own ethos, its own history, its own sense of its citizenry and what it can get away with; its own traditions and above all, perhaps, its own economics. In neo-colonialism, which is the new enslavement of people in all parts of the world, this involves atrocious international connections, multi-national companies, the links between the slaves in the mines and the slaves in the factories and the good life here, in the taxation system, etc., etc. So the translation here is the task, the translation as in our country is the task.

There is a very fine line that we try to walk, all of us in our communities, between being fundamentalists in an obsessive way (that is to say 'everything is evil and keep away'), and on the other hand reading it in the ordinary kind of liberal religious way which always says 'nothing applies, it's all abstract, there is no disturbance really worth our own sweat or tears, there is nothing really happening that should shake us in our institutions or in our communities or our churches, etc., etc.'

Somewhere between there, it seems to me, the issue has to be pushed home. Our tragedy is that so few have been able to do this. Probably your tragedy is that so few have been able to understand the longer-term educational task of understanding some of the things that Bishop Winter brought up the other day. He has been a kind of traveller between enslavement abroad and the pseudo 'good life' here and understands those links because he sees the other end of the problem. In any case I would submit that the attempt of the state to claim us is total, whether it takes the brutal direct military form or the more indirect economic form. The tendency of the state is always in the direction of that totalization of service, which comes to rest, of course, in the metaphor or the fact of total war. It is total war upon the human spirit and the human community, and the only path towards integrity lies in those discussions we have been having so passionately and so constantly during these days, i.e. the creation of alternatives to this, so that one need not live off the misery of others. One tries to have only the most indirect and tenuous connection with that life which demands death at the other end. One refuses to disappear within the state as another element of its so-called 'life'. One refuses to disappear there, as a good passive integer who has been stamped 'grade A'.

I could not think of a society on the face of the earth today to which our reflections would not apply. More especially (you don't want to go abroad and mystify our situation), more especially it seems to me to be impossible for Christians in the *West* to think that these reflections do not apply to their states. The state is not the Beast in the sense of the book, that is always overtly devouring in a crude manner. The book is more subtle about the nature of the thing, which nature, it would seem to me, we are in a much better position to understand than those early Christians, because we have had to live with it longer and we have now a long history of the Beast to draw upon. Let me just conclude by suggesting that there are two or three tendencies that the book would have us alive to in this conception of the state.

First of all we have often talked about the question of violence. The state – that conglomeration of authority and power – is innately violent, whether or not it is overtly violent on this or that occasion. It can live by violence and exist by violence. Therefore those who oppose it and do not expect violence are gulls. Therefore those who oppose the state and can offer no alternative, are fools. The state, for its own existence, demands the police and the FBI, and if it is an international reality, as ours – the CIA and the Special Branches and the new technology, and the third and fourth generation of anti-personnel weaponry and a creation of conflict around the world based upon economic needs, and therefore the continuous renewal of its military machine, into more and more atrocious forms of anti-human action and weaponry. So that will be the first fact, the fact of violence and the meaning of that for us who are within the state in a very special way, obviousiy, as Christians.

Number two: could I speak of something else which needs a little more subtlety, but I think people here will get the point? It is something like 'distraction', or maybe it can be translated 'insanity', or maybe in the sense of some of the British experiments and communes in dealing with disturbed people, 'schizophrenia', though of course a lot of people have thrown that word out now. (T. S. Eliot was very attached to the word 'distraction'. Remember he defined modern life, especially urban life, as 'people who are distracted from distraction by distraction'. Like you, he had a sense of being pulled aside from the true task, from reality.) Put the word in that expresses profound moral and intellectual derangement; I don't know. It is that mentality which in our society locks up victims who emotionally cannot cope, and allows the most atrocious criminality at the highest levels of authority, day after day. It is not merely the fact that there is a kind of victimized insanity at the bottom of the heap and a kind of totally inhuman insanity rampant at the top. It is the relationship between these things that we are trying to understand. So that the question of the Book of Revelation at this point, I would suggest, for us is, 'What form or power is the truth to come from?' Or to be very concrete about it, 'How does one stay sane in insane surroundings.?'

This is a question that comes now with a particular horror upon the Vietnamese people and with another kind of subtle horror upon us. How to retain some sort of spiritual integrity, some sort of ability to move and to function as a being with something above the shoulders, when practically everything we were born to believe has come in doubt? When practically every one of those structures we could lean upon as we were meant to, as human beings, to guideposts, to medicine, to law, to health, to school, to churches, are coming down? What the state or the Beast is supplying for us is that kind of omnivorous metaphor of the structure that is devouring instead of serving. How to come upon the truth, and upon sanity, and function within all that and not give up, not give up? Of course the definition of the state and the cry that issues from the litter of the Beast is 'Give up, give up.'

I think we have been trying to explore those alternatives during these days. I think we have been trying to say something important and very previous about our local communities, our common pool of sanity upon which we can draw, and draw and move and be available and be patient and be cheerful, and endure the long haul. And escape, sometimes by laughter, sometimes by tears and sometimes by patience, and by all those hallmarks of sanity, escape all the seductions of insanity that are calling us. So we have concluded (at least I thought we had) that our communities are very important to us; that the fostering of a sense of mystery among ourselves is important; that the celebration of this sense of things at times, through the eucharist, common prayer, through our scriptures, through good deals, through all kinds of means is very important; and that our politics will avoid that dreadful narrowing of spirit and hardening of heart to which the society itself invites us, and will keep open-minded and open-hearted and compassionate among ourselves in the measure in which we can keep these living communities going. Maybe we have come to understand that the kind of sanity we are trying to speak of and understand is a profoundly personal self-possession that is only possible because it is a community possession. The very shape of our society urges that truth upon us – that we survive in proportion as we build together – that we die in proportion as the state in all its forms, in all its movements on us, is able to isolate us and work us over with its own special tools of despair and distraction, and long-handed power, and soft- and hardware and all the rest. So that's about it, I think so far as I am concerned. I hope that many of us can take home what I would be very grateful for, that is, a new sense from the very large and wide experience that we have shared, and our background, a new sense of what we can do and what we can be, *together*.

PART TWO

Stony Ground

WHERE IS COMMUNITY?

Discussion with Dan Berrigan

Q/C★   Why do you think they let you out?

D.B.   Oh, I don't know, the Beast is clever, but not that clever. They also let Phil (Berrigan) out after 39 months in prison, about five days before Christmas, and he's now saying these things, and better, all across his scene too. So they are always stuck with people like ourselves; they don't know what to do. If you're in gaol you're dangerous, and if you're outside you're dangerous. So they try both.

Q/C   How can you condemn the state so completely, if the state is made up of people?

D.B.   I can only suggest that our experience right now is probably important to a lot of people since they live and die according to American decisions. That the state is the prime source of disorder rather than order. That in introducing disorder into every facet of life, from the courts to the police, to the gaols, to the universities, indeed to the churches – the church establishment at least, and that the dissolution of that historical role as the source of order is one of the ways of putting the facts of the times. That the state, which at various times has revealed itself by its own prescripts as the source of human order and law and justice, reveals another side entirely about these. And not only tells the truth suddenly about itself in the B.52s over the cities, but works towards the destruction of all those sub-groupings, those professional groupings within the state which in better times would be serving people. That even medicine, education and religion become tools of the larger disorder and become captivated by its mystique and in Beast-like kind of silence, join the Great Cry. This is what we are witnessing.

It is very difficult in our society to find even a small grouping, that

★ Q/C = question/comment.

is a traditional grouping, a professional grouping, a religious grouping that is in any real sense serving people, unless it has been born in the last ten years, or unless those older things have reassembled in the last ten years. There are such caucuses at the edge of the traditional groupings. And so we find our lawyers have to reassemble to serve the poor. We find our doctors have to reassemble and do studies with a new kind of powerlessness, for new forms, new powers to serve the poor. We find our young clergy have to do the same thing. Similarly with students . . . etc. Because the larger groupings have become complicit with the larger crimes, at least by silence. And here we could go into the whole question of the church, obviously, but you know it as well as I do.

Q/C   Would you say that the state sometimes covers itself with the odour of respectability of the institutionalized church and therefore makes it a party and colludes with it so that the church itself gets rich benefits from vested interests in it? I think the tragic result is to find a few isolated priests or ministers like Cosmas Desmond who can easily be isolated from the church.

D.B.   I don't know if that even requires comment. I have one minor objection. I think that anyone who sets out on a course of truth and truthful action in any profession or any phase of life is a fool and should have stayed where he was if he is allowing himself to be isolated. You get what I mean? We were never isolated. Let me recall the record. We were never isolated except in a very dolorous and very brief first stage which was to be expected. If you are going to take illegal action on behalf of people, for a while people are going to get shocked about what you do, especially in a country like ours, but if the action was right there is a very speedy reintegration of con-sciousness around what you do, and then it becomes very precious, a reworking of the times. But you see, suppose one or another of us, Philip or any of the original Nine, had decided that he was as an individual going to do this thing alone. There would have been a catastrophe instead. So that the work of tactic, which is always very captivating to people in bad times – 'What is the tactic?' – that is in itself a captivation. The first question is, 'Where is the community?' and then out of the community comes naturally the tactic. It doesn't even have to be asked if the community is genuine.

With regards to the gentleman's question. If this natural order of things is preserved, it seems to me that the heart of the thing will be the opposite of isolation. Because the nine of us went through this thing together, reasonably together, we could wait for the thing to gather steam, we could wait for ourselves to be welcomed or – rejected. We could face either outcome and both happened of course. I could not stress too strongly that in our experience part of the inner tragedy of resistance is the isolation of people who never really got together in their own souls about their lives and then were very easily broken as a consequence.

Q/C   I wonder if there are others like me, who never really thought like this before, and find it really helpful, but who feel attracted to the comments of my friend from South Africa over here.★ I would like to make two points. Number one, although I have never thought about it before, it seems very important for us to analyse what we mean by the state. Do we mean any group of people who have control over other people and who are violent and deceitful and demand a kind of religious awe? Because then it isn't simply the Tory or the Labour Party in this country, but it's all sorts of institutions. To emphasize the state means that we ignore similar corrupt institutions elsewhere. Number two, I wonder if it is indeed people with power over other persons that do these things. If it is not a kind of biological problem, in that when humans get together in such a way that they have power over others, this tends to be, but not always, a product. In which case I am a little lost as to what we do. Do we really expect a perpetual renewal or do we act as individuals acting in some sort of disorganized way with other people?

Q/C   Perhaps I could offer a definition of the power of the state which wouldn't be too abstract, but which could relate to our personal lives. I think it was a Marxist, if it was not an anarchist, who defined the state as 'the organization of violence'; quite a useful definition. But how is the power of violence organized in the state? To me it seems to operate on three levels, what you might call: 1. armed force; 2. productive force; 3. ideological force. Within that we can categorize all sorts of institutions: the education system, medical welfare system, as well as the police and the gaols and the courts and so on. In fact one could get down to the biological system of the family grouping, to include in a sense the power of violence which would be a force of life, a biological force. That would mean what the women in Women's Lib. talk about when they say that the power of male authority is a natural authority insofar as it is biological to him, and therefore to abolish that authority you have to change all sorts of things which even we as radical politicos and radical Christians accept as natural. I want to raise one issue that has

★ Second question above.

47

not been raised before, the problem of sexuality. Because as products of the Christian tradition and of the revolutionary political tradition, I would submit for discussion that our sexuality is being suppressed and it may be that sexuality is the missing link that could bridge the gap between life and love, religion and politics, matter and spirit. It is difficult to talk about sexuality, because it affects our deepest emotions and therefore our own religious emotions, but it is also a very material thing, as you know, and certainly the Popes of this world and the Stalins of this world know that sexual dignities equal political impetus. People on the Left, both political and religious, are beginning to talk about connections between sexual potence and political liberation, stemming from the work of Reich, Marcuse and so on. I wonder if we could talk about that.* I don't know if the group is too big to talk about that; I don't know if that is what you meant about the power of one person over another, perhaps you mean biological. Perhaps it would make sense to read into that the more traditional theory about the state, and about economics and so on.

Q/C   We are not biologically conditioned. Our consciousness is formed by our situation in Britain and yet we in Britain do not see the Beast. He is still so comfortably at home that we do not recognize his existence. This is obvious in the significant lack of response, the inability of the few who burn the Beast in our situation to get the response to this most cynical attitude of Nixon and the war machine in the States. There has been very little response over here, as you know. It is this difficulty that I am concerned with. The Beast is all-absorbing over here, just as it is in the States. Those of us who have tried to fight against it over the last few years have found that so. Yet in a sense it is frustrating in a different way, that we can find no place to be, to transform what is. We can find no way of purging the Beast, and yet there is no consciousness that there *is* a Beast. The Beast is still able to thrive softly and quietly. Another problem is that the kind of radicalism in the States is not present here, even though there is a much deeper class confrontation in Britain at this very moment. That is significant. Yet the class confrontation is not one in which most people in this room are very consciously involved. It is very fundamental to our society. The tragedy is – as one who has been involved in this confrontation at its roots for several years, in rent strikes, and so forth can see – the tragedy is, in the vast confrontation there is little consciousness that what we are opposing is a Beast in which we are still involved, even though we are opposing it.

In this situation we are beginning to recognize, even if it's a new

* An additional group was arranged to take up this issue.

thing, a new idea, we are beginning to see that the state and all its implications is the enemy. How do we begin to get at all its absorbing structures of power and domination, to create a new society, a new style of resistance, a new community? The great hope which throughout the Western world seemed to be there has disintegrated. The Left parties have grown, but not very much. Beyond them there are no new structures of living with any coherence. That is our situation, at least as I see it.

Q/C   Talking about the Beast, you have depersonalized it, and yet as the last speaker pointed out, most of us are involved in the Beast and are part of the Beast. This seems to me to suggest that the centre of our new community must be a religious one, a spiritual one. Whatever I do I am a part of it too, and therefore a perpetual spiritual renewal is needed.

D.B.   I was wondering whether or not it was possible in the light of either the British or American experience to do anything but depersonalize the state, as the state has depersonalized itself, and whether our attitude toward it is accurate or distorted. It seems to me that one must deal with what has actually happened. I want to be very concrete about it. In our significant, conscious lifetime it has been practically impossible to find in any highly-placed government official, any human response to the realities of the world. One might say the same thing of those at the top echelon of sub-groupings, including the church. It is, after ten years of war, practically impossible to talk to any of the American cardinals or bishops. So that we are confronted with a conception of authority or power, whether sacred or secular, which progressively has depersonalized those who wanted it. I wanted to place this in perspective because of ourselves. It seems to me the gospel allows for, encourages and even confers, announces, the gift of a new kind of power which is rather a deeper personalization or socialization – these are aspects of the same thing – rather than the process which is immemorially that of this world, to destroy that which counts to the point where the thing that we spoke of is the ordinary commerce of the top, that is to say, to seek violence and demand a religious awe or response. It is practically impossible in the Western world, and quite rare in the Marxist world, to find the possession of power joined to an acute human sense. I mean any society within the echelon of competence. So it seems to me that an investigation of a new kind of power, a new kind of authority, is also of great import. Because as several have hinted here this morning, the Beast is also within, and the enticement into the methodology and the mystique of this world is very powerful to those who would oppose it or confront it. We very often notice that the same inhumanity and violence is blatant in the Left of which they have accused the Right. Even though, as several also have noticed, the need of a constant renewal and verification is obviously very great.

Q/C   Can I take up this point about violence and non-violence? You seem to hold that change can be non-violent. You referred to China as another Beast, and now there is this thing about the reaction of the Left being violence. Surely the problem is of some kind of time-scale. If, for instance in China, the poor and the oppressed people had decided to change things non-violently, would they have been changed by now? What is the situation about Vietnam? What is the hope in terms of Vietnam, of kicking out the Americans, or in terms of the Vietnamese waiting for non-violent change within the United States to get the Americans to withdraw from Vietnam? I am a bit sceptical about non-violence in the short term, and the things that you might dislike about the violence on the Left perhaps can be the only response in the short term to save lives, to relieve the oppressed and try and change the situation to another situation which perhaps, although it itself needs changing, at least in the short term, is preferable to the previous situation.

D.B.   I think one of the difficulties about our conference is to try and keep our topics workable. Everything opens up a vast world to discussion and talk. I find it personally difficult to get into a discussion on the effectiveness of non-violence in the world at large. I think, though, to narrow the question, that I would like to apply it to Britain as well as America. The dolorous experience of ten years is that violence is another stereotype in our society, that they always have more guns than we, presupposing we want guns, and that those elements of the Left which have gone in for violence have been very quickly and very efficiently destroyed. So that our question has been one of tactic as well as belief, and I would find it difficult to say when the one begins and the other ends. You see, from the many points of view, including the presence of many Third-World people in our midst, who helped and joined with us, it was clear that even if they did not share our religious convictions they shared our tactical under-standing, that violence within our highly charged technological society was suicidal, and that for us there could be no other way except that of non-violent change. I submit that probably the same is true here.

Q/C   I think that, as I understand our topic, we are here to ask what our resources are and what our tactics are in the society we live in, confronting the state as we know it, without any implication that we cannot learn from elsewhere, but not trying to get into a huge kind of world mix-up of 'what works and what doesn't work', etc. – worse still a kind of bravado of East versus West. I would like to leave here a little less ignorant about how we can survive psychologically and spiritually as the struggle goes on.

Q/C   I am a little concerned about the over-emphasis on the state. First of all, the suggestion that the state is all-powerful, that it is Nixon and that it is Heath who are in control of our society. Secondly, the assumption that the state as such is a wholly malevolent institution. I believe that over-simplifies the whole question a great deal. For I am pretty certain that the state is part of the whole duality that exists within our society. The state represents a tool on behalf of the capitalist class. But at the same time I believe that due to the struggles of the workers and the oppressed peoples we have been able to make some advances within that system. We had somebody talk about the educational system and the social welfare system and many other systems that the state sets up. We are talking about alternatives, but when I seriously think about the sort of alternative state I want and the distinct elements of everybody's alternative state in this room, I am very certain that at the end of it we will have an aggregate state that in some circumstances could be just as frightening as anything else that anyone else could provide. What I would like to suggest is that our situation is not as hopeless as this room today has come to think. You know the smiles have gradually fallen off our faces as we move around the depressive stage of our schizophrenic cycle. I think that if we are serious about changing society, if we are serious about seeking alternatives, then we have to do one thing, and one very important thing, and that is to look at what other people who are within the system, within the state, within the society are saying. Look, for example, at what the Marxists are saying – and I don't mean when we look at the Marxists that we have a Christian-Marxist dialogue, a country conference type of thing. Let us do what Lenin said – and he is always good to quote around these places; nobody else knows what he said, anyway – that 'an ounce of experience is worth a ton of theory'. What I would say we have to do here, if we are going to do anything relevant, is to go and talk with other elements in our society, progressive elements who are trying to do things to change the society, and by this I *do* mean the Communist Party and the Labour Party and the Trade Union Movement. You may laugh at the idea of talking to the Labour Party, but there are some very nice people in the Labour Party. I believe that in the Labour Party and in the working class movements, *there* is the grave-digger of capitalism. I believe that we can overthrow capitalism, for capitalism is full of contradictions and the contradiction of the state is the working-class movements. This is what we have got to do, and this is where our hope should be, if we are to advance – if we are to get beyond wishy-washy liberalism.

Q/C How would you feel about changing the structure of this conference into having a thought-shop tomorrow, the day after an action-shop, and the day after that a reflection shop/revolutionary shop, and to go on from there? This would be to get away from talking, which is a form of self-indulgence. How long have we been thinking about these problems, though, let's think about it tomorrow and action the day after that. (*Aside:* the Kingdom on Monday.)

Q/C I come from Northern Ireland. Do you not think that in the struggle against what you call the state, when you have tried other methods, in the end you are left with no other option but to use violence as at least a beginning to bring about a solution or an answer to the problem? You see, I come from Belfast and this is the idea put out by the people who are responsible for the violence in Northern Ireland. For a long time (I use the Civil Rights movement as an example), they tried other methods and got nowhere, except beaten down into the ground. They got absolutely no response except that the whole machinery of the state organized itself to suppress it. They now argue that the only answer up there is to use violence so that the state will have to move and do something.

D.B. Obviously there is no answer to a problem like that except in terms of the people and their resources that are there. But on the other hand, I do not want to leave it there, because I feel that my tradition has something to say to historical violence and enough to give one pause under the most intense provocation. First of all, could I say something that all of us have tried to share in the last few years, that non-violence is not a tool for preaching, and it is not a weapon against the oppressed people, otherwise we are back to colonialism where the missioners could be brought in with the soldiers to say to the natives, 'Will you grovel?' We are all familiar with those stereotypes. On the other hand, one can speak about a very long and difficult experience in one's own society which perhaps may have something to say to other people, and other societies, that will give us pause. We are not Vietnamese, and we are not oppressed Third-World people, and part of the intense obsessive alienation of many American movements has been this attempt to identify with Marxism and with the Viet-Cong and all the rest of it. It has been turned into a charade, a joke, and was extremely easy to deal with on the part of the police, the FBI, the army and all the other facilities at hand. It is very important to see ourselves where we are, concretely and modestly, and to see who and what we are not and to make very tentatively those identifications with Third-World people or with Belfast people or any kind of people who are under the guns. We must try to live in such a way that we try with every bit of resource and heart and brain we have, to create something beside guns as a way of life. The American example is the making of violence into the ordinary political message, so that the decibel, the body count is the measure of political advance. This is a horrible and creeping disease which has permeated the society almost totally. I must say from the point of view of that blood-ridden society, that I find violence historically uninteresting. I can only speak for my own society, but it is some society, and those gun barrels are very long and they find easily dispensable a lot of people of the world, with no clear distinction between Third World and Second World, etc., when the chips are down. I think it would be extremely profitable for people to reflect on this aspect of things. The trouble with us (and by us I mean Westerners in general) is this extreme impoverishment of the imagination, so that many of us will declare before we even try that non-violence has failed, because we have never had the wit and the depth to explore what it might mean, and that is the failure of our movement, as I know bitterly night and day. That we are not Vietnamese, and that we do not have their resources, and that we are not Buddhists, and we do not have their resources, and that as Christians in the West we share the general bankruptcy of moral means and the general itch toward immoral means. So that a gathering in the States is constantly edging away from what might be called true purpose and true hope and true alternatives – dragging in the world, and especially the violence of the world at large, as its ruling metaphor. How difficult it is for us, and I presume also for you, to grant any place to the question of non-violent alternatives in our own societies. How difficult and how rare it is to stay with those questions as though they were real questions.

Spiritually speaking, most of us are usually armed, in the sense that the metaphors of arms and violence rule our thought and our speech, because that is what is up close at our own doors and that's what we are born with, and that is our real baptism.

53

Q/C   I live in a situation in Belfast where violence is quite literally on our doorsteps. The question I would like to ask is, when you destroy a state, however corrupt, what does this lead to? I can assure you that it is very much less pleasant to live with a non-state than any state. The state might well have been corrupt, but when it is destroyed we are left with dreadful chaos for three years. As you all know, four hundred and fifty people have died in this year, and hundreds more have been terribly maimed. We are literally living packed together by the fear of a gunman or a bomb coming to our door. The resistance against our government started as a peace movement and has always maintained that its end was peace. Violence came later, I believe. I can say that the vast majority of people in Northern Ireland are moderate and they want a peaceful solution. They want a just solution. But I think that the most terrible thing in our situation is that we just do not seem to see any solution, and I think that this is what is grinding to a halt any pacifist response, and leading to distress and despair. Everything has been tried, but the moderates just do not seem to have a chance. It is a very frustrating situation to be living in when you just do not see any solution and you do not know what will come tomorrow. So I will say that if you are going to destroy a state, if you are going to be destructive, you have to be constructive as well.

D.B.   Can I say this, that I find the phrase 'destruction of the state' is relative to our position and our needs. In the States I find it totally unrealistic; it has nothing to do with what we are trying to do. It is a kind of alienated rhetoric that keeps people from the real job. The real job is knowing that in your lifetime you are going to have very small things to do locally with a few people about change, and that the accretion of thousands, many many myriads of change might bring real change. In the meantime you are trying to live as though a future were possible and as though local models could be enlarged and that is about all. Once people get abstract on big jobs, I run for the window.

DEVELOPING THE ALTERNATIVE
Discussion with Jim Forest

Q/C Jim, could you talk a bit about your communities and their relation to the state?

J.F. First of all, we do not work for the state, we do not pay taxes, we do not fill out their forms, we do not ask for their privileges and we try as much as possible to decentralize, because the power of the state is very much a consequence of the centralization process, and we try to move in the opposite direction. We try to dramatize that by pruning as much as possible from the relationship. Obviously there is no way to be absolutely pure, absolutely untouched by realities we do not care for. We sometimes use cars, we sometimes use aeroplanes; we use money; we use the telephone.

Q/C That's all right for people like you and a few people who are in the movement who are helped by the movement. It's all right for people who maybe for the next few years will work for a movement here. What about the large percentage of people here, who are going to have to go out and get jobs? They cannot decide whether they want jobs or not.

J. F. First of all, many of us have jobs. We tried to get away from this old movement clericalism where those very holy radicals had to pass the hat to people who were not so holy and say, 'Say, please give us some of your ill-gotten goods to keep us holy ones going.' The term 'bread labour' has come up in the American movement. We really are trying to find ways of simply being examples of how anybody could step outside the consumer-addicting syndrome and live simply and do useful things that are important to other people and be sustained by that. I think we look back on a movement that is very much like the worst aspects of mediaeval Catholicism. 'We Monsignors and bishops and cardinals, and so forth, are to pass a collection basket all the time because "we have the truth and you guys don't, and we are sacrificing more".' You have to keep a very grim face for this process, because if you start getting happy and having fun, well this changes the whole reality of the situation, and people don't empty their wallets so quickly.

Q/C   How do you work out the tension between creating an alternative way of doing things and working within the system?

J.F.   The experience that I have been involved in and been a part of is that we are involved in both areas. The point is to create new things for people who are ready and to make ourselves available where people are not ready. I have a friend who is fourteen years old who had an opportunity of going to a local Free School. He chose not to, because he said that most of his friends were not ready for that, and that he would rather carry on the struggle in their school. He thought this was much more in the spirit of resistance, not just to 'create some kind of Utopia' as he put it rather contemptuously, but to be where other kids were. I am not as uptight as he was about going off and creating free schools, especially if they *are* open, such as the First Street School, just down the road from the Catholic Worker, that has been described in *The Lives of Children*. It was free to the neighbourhood and the reason it went under was because they were insistent that they would allow kids to come whether or not their parents had any money. They finally just could not keep going because nobody in the neighbourhood had any money – it was ninety per cent welfare. So I think it is not one or the other. Very quickly we find ourselves working out of both corners – which confuses people and makes it a little harder for them to announce in the *New York Times* exactly what we are about.

Q/C   Can I ask you to articulate something which may be very difficult. That is, going back to Matthew 25, 'in as much as you did these things unto the least of mine, you did these things to me'. Now I expect most people can understand very clearly how Jesus demands of us our care for the oppressed. Yet how in the light of that sort of thinking and teaching, and in the light of your own experience, can you actually say that you see Jesus in the hungry and the naked, etc., etc.?

J.F.   I would not dare say that I see Jesus in the hungry and the naked. He tells me that he is there, that is clear. God knows, I am alive when I am involved in these things. Perhaps I see Jesus in those

moments when I am alive, but at those moments when I am alive
I become less reflective about what it is to be alive. I move out of that
kind of state where I am looking into the present and see in what is
happening, and analysing it. 'Ahem, Jesus is there' . . . you know. I
just think of the Buddhist story of the young fellow who asked the
Zen master, 'Master, what should I do if I see the Buddha on the
street?' The Zen master says, 'If you see the Buddha, kill him.'

It's a very scary thing to meditate on, because we really want to
encapsulate our God experience into imagining that sooner or later,
like taking the underground, we are going to get to that station, 'the
God experience' – we will know it and we will have placards on the
wall and we will have arrived and we don't have to go on from there.
God is usually kept in that kind of subway station analogy. But the
model is nonsense. If we want a model, we had better think instead
of the game of hide and seek; except that as soon as we get to home
base we find that home base has moved. This is how the whole
death and rebirth thing becomes vivid to me and why I relate to the
whole idea of resurrection so profoundly; when I get some supposed final goal and find it's not *the* place, there is a kind of awful
collapse. Then in that collapse I discover that I am on the way again,
and *that* is being there; being there is to be on the way. It is full of
puzzles and contradictions and ironies and paradoxes, but it is the only
experience of God that I can begin to talk about, and it's a kind of
non-experience.

Q/C   Can you talk a bit about your relation to the eucharist?

J.F.   I am a terribly weird mixture of terribly conservative traditional
things side by side with things which are apparently not very traditional at the moment. I like being at the eucharist with anybody who
wants to be there, for example, but I also enjoy going to churches
with people who, it would seem on the surface, do not have too much
of an idea of what the whole thing is about. At the same time there
are times when I have to gather around bread and wine with people
with whom I am living and working. It would be just inconceivable
that we would get together without that kind of happening.

Q/C   What about the first kind of people to whom you do not have
to relate much?

J.F.   I feel that there is a tremendous relation going on there. It is a
hidden relation, it's not overt, it's implied by our space and by our
hope. Really it throws me right back into the present time in an

important way because I find it easy to hide out with people who share similar understandings and to hear things that I like to hear that reassure me, but I couldn't remain sane without these experiences of people who think I am crazy.

Q/C   Does the eucharist make you stronger?

J.F.   I don't know; when you make love, does it make you stronger? I don't know. I hope so. It is like the whole thing of daring to try out silence or daring to try out a lot of things that are outside of the culture that 'don't make sense' (which I usually think is spelt *cents*). It's just been such a long time since I could imagine living without these 'insane' follies of imagining that God is hidden in the taste of bread as well as in everything else. That he is there. God is there – then where is God not? If God is willing to identify with this . . .?

Q/C   But is he in the state as well?

J.F.   The word 'state' is a word we have invented. Some of the words we have invented I like, but state is not one of them, although it is an an inevitable outgrowth of what people have tried to pull off, the rip-off. The state is one of those words that descends from the earliest tradition of people ripping other people off and giving it nice names, like 'tactical responses', instead of 'bombing village'. The state is a synonym for the Mafia. The Mafia is an Americanization for our kind of organized body for crime.
   The state is something that we agree exists, but we could agree does not exist just as simply and with a great sigh of relief. So I would rather talk about community. It seems to me that community is a possibly real world, and that is the direction that I would like to see us move. It's a word that is built on the assumption that it's possible for people to relate to each other in non-manipulative non-coercive ways, and that states as we know them historically are absolutely tied to the tradition of fear – manipulation – greed – coercion – violence – killing.

Q/C   What is the difference between the state and the mechanism by which you would arrange for a family so many thousand miles away to get some help in a very complicated society?

J.F.   I think it is a matter of difference of motive. If we want to talk about the state, then we talk about those communities where people assist one another for manipulative purposes and with manipulative and vile intents. We are a community that seems to be responsible for human beings, it seems to me, for a completely different constellation of motives. That motive might happen to do with the fact that you value what you are doing, even though there is no way of being employed except by us. We have that in our communities. We have some people who work as nurses, some people writing, some people who wash dishes and cook meals and make money. We have people that we plead with not to do these things because we want to have them twenty-four hours a day doing something that nobody is going to pay them for except us. So the community becomes the 'employer', though we do not ever use the term. That is the difference.

Q/C   Can I take you up on what you have just said? You employ people like nurses?

J.F.   We have people in the community who make money by doing things like that.

Q/C   Sorry, I thought you mentioned something about not paying taxes at one point. How do you not pay taxes if you are employed as a nurse?

J.F.   Sometimes they take the money. We do not consider that paying taxes. We consider that being robbed. But let me give you the example of a teacher at a little college in California. She put down on a US form that she had five or six dependents, which meant that she was not eligible to have taxes taken out due to the number of dependents she had. She claimed these dependents because she had five or six Vietnamese kids who were living there in a house that she had rented and they were completely economically dependent on her. They were in the US for major surgery, the rebuilding of melted faces, and shattered jaws and multiple breaks in the spinal column and things of that kind. They were her dependents even though the tax people are still threatening to send her to prison because they are not American citizens and she is not giving the money through a tax exempt foundation and she has no right to do those things except through the housebroken charities.
  She is continuing to do that, and every once in a while the government grabs into her bank account and takes her car and sells it at an auction. But that is stealing, that's not paying taxes. We know that we get stolen from, we know that we cannot stop these robbers coming into the house, but we do not invite them in and tell them to sit down and make themselves comfortable while we write out a cheque.

Q/C   Can I briefly be the devil's advocate? I don't know quite if
you are actually ordained or anything else, but my reaction is, 'Okay,
it's all right for him, he is a priest, he is a drop-out, you know, he is
safe in his own community, he can work among the oppressed and
he can talk about the oppressed and he knows who they are, they are
the blacks, they are the starving.' You know it's so bloody easy. In that
film we saw the other night, *Punishment Park*, who were the oppressed
there? Were they the kids who were being shot? I don't think they
were. They were the people who were in the uniforms, they were
the people who were on the draft boards, and the point is, is our
message merely for the blacks, or for the starving, or the people
whom it's easy to see are oppressed? If our message is to mean anything, it's got to mean something to the people who are on the
housing estates, the posh people, the middle-class housing estates.

J.F.   The only thing puzzling to me about that is that you thought
that that was a devil's advocate statement. I must have communicated
very badly because I couldn't agree with you more. The only thing
I would add to that is that it seems to me that not only the police are
oppressed, though they are. Not just that the draft board members are
oppressed, though most certainly they are being stripped dreadfully
of any of the human potential that is in them waiting to grow, and
it's being done in a systematic, ruthless and sinister way, and has been
for a long time – and that is oppression. I would add that I do not
recall ever having met somebody whom I didn't think in some way
was oppressed. It seems to me that the forms the oppression takes
become more or less violent, though essentially they are all violent.
There is a kind of polite violence, something like an open security
prison, and they allow you to go there because they are quite certain
you will not walk away. So they don't need the wall. Why spend the
money on the wall if you put up your own wall for them in your
brain? So I agree, but I am *distressed about a movement that gets involved
in, as I said before, clericalism or elitism*, and that figures out one group
of people who are oppressed and everyone else is not, for it seems to
me that is a kind of blindness.

Q/C   You see, Lenin said something that I think is very relevant –
and I quote Lenin again. He said, 'I would wear a top hat for the
revolution if I thought it would advance the cause of the working-
class.' Sometimes I have spoken to that vanguard of the revolutionary
movement, Women's Institutes, and I have turned up and spoken to
them, looking something like I look now, which is pretty alien to
them, and I've said, 'Ladies, there is something wrong with society.'

Immediately they say, 'No, absolute rubbish.' But if you shave your beard off and cut your hair and wear a white shirt and tie, you can have far more impact. You've got to be a Trojan horse. The Bible talks about causing stumbling blocks to people, and the trouble is with us, with our 'trendy Leftism', as your workers see it when they meet your long haired bloke who is living on Social Security and ask, 'What does that long-haired bloke on Social Security really know about what it is like to go to work and to have to provide for three kids and have to pay a higher rent? He does not, he cannot understand. How can what he says be relevant to us who have to be part of the system, who have to strike?' This is the whole point of it, we have got to do away with the stumbling block. We have got to have the courage, and say that God is so sufficient that if this is your particular type of witness, we can actually live on a suburban housing estate. We can actually do the pilgrimage both ways, but we can do something useful and something real in terms of changing our society and building the type of society we really want. We must have that courage. If we have not had that courage, then we have failed, and this is the whole point of it. If you want to know, if you really want to go away from this conference with something worth while, think on this, 'How are we going to liberate the English middle-class of whom most of us are members?' If you can come up with a solution to that, you will come up with one of the most profound things that is going to affect this country. Please think about it.

Q/C   I want to know how far you are going to cut your hair and shave off your moustache and all that sort of thing, because I go out addressing Women's Institutes and the Rotary Club and things like that and I think you have to work out a compromise. You see, ultimately, if you take their arguments to their logical conclusions, you will end up part of the system. Look at all those God-fearing Socialists who went into the Labour Movement at the beginning of this century and ended up in a top-hat and tails and going to Buckingham Palace in '24 and whose sons then became Tory MPs, and things like that. You have got to watch that. On the other hand, you are quite right, if you go with very long hair and all that, you turn them right off. I think you have to compromise. They have got to see that you are different. If you go looking like them, you will end up speaking like them. You will have an 'Animal Farm' again. It is very very difficult to stay down the middle. The question I want to put to you is on the whole question of the line that he is drawing. You say you do not pay taxes, yet we know they do pay taxes. I do not mind to a certain extent paying some taxes. I do not mind paying for hospital services because I don't have the 'know-how' to be a surgeon, etc. But am I like hell paying taxes for the defence and for mis-education. This question of bread-earning . . . What jobs are there? There are only a limited number of jobs that we can do that can earn bread. I have racked my brains over this. I am trained as a teacher, yet some people say, 'Why don't you be a part-time teacher?' But I can't, because as soon as I become involved in a job I want to put everything I have into it, and then I have no time for anything else, and I think that most of the other jobs we are doing are going to be like that or they are going to be bum jobs like working in a factory line. I could not stand that. How many jobs are open to us on this whole question of bread? How much time have we left to serve the revolution?

J.F.   Well, first let me just comment on the Trojan horse versus the Galilean donkey. I would suggest that it is not just 'who we should be' but trying to discover 'who we actually are' that is important. Some of us are people who are disinterested in the clothing and the trapping and the hybrid vocabularies and so forth. Our most urgent nature is to be with people who need us and to be with them as they need us. You know the gospel that we read aloud in the silence today, 'to bring good news to the poor'. I have always thought it rather un-fortunate that we have never asked the poor what they would consider to be good news. I think part of the good news is going to people in a way that they can hear us, but I do not want to do that as a kind of circus barker thing when I am actually detesting people, that would be like selling tickets to the side-show muttering 'suckers' between sales. I want to be with people in a way that springs out of my guts. I want to be there because I respect and understand these people and I *want* to be with them. But if I am the kind of person, on the other hand, who feels that my business is not going to be so much in verbal things or organizing, but a way of life and making a kind of circus of my body, that's great. People stare at me, are puzzled by me. That's one way of dealing with and affecting other people's realities, and I think that what we have learnt in our experience with the more contemplative members of our community, like Thomas Merton, is that there is nothing that we accomplish until we are willing to go through the crisis of trying to find out 'who I am' instead of 'how can I be what other people want me to be?' Whether it be Dorothy Day or Daniel Berrigan or some great radical, or people in charge of these institutions. I don't want anybody to be the engineer of my life and to tell me what my conscience ought to be saying. I want to find out for myself, frightening as it may be. The only kind of communities

I respect are those that do not have models for members to squeeze into, but which are willing to try to help members listen to what one's conscience might have to say about how to be alive and how to listen, and how to communicate. So it's not so much a matter of rejecting being a Trojan horse. Some people can do that because as it might be said in other traditions, 'that's their karma'. But I would not want to make a system of it, as I think one of the words for violence is *system*. I don't want people to be good machines that will 'make the revolution' by being machines in any automobile factory. I want our communities to be something different from that, because we are not trying to be like machines, we are not suffering from machine envy.

The whole business of taxes – I don't want to get hung up about that. I just offered it as a kind of symbol, or a sign or a ritual that it seems to me is connected to the business of trying to pronounce something on the state. I am simply intent not to condemn militarism and its domestic equivalent while I am meanwhile writing my cheque out; by subsidizing those things I feel that there would be some contradiction there and that people would have a right to be puzzled. Thus our communities have looked for ways somehow to resist taxes. There is not *a* way of resisting taxes but thousands of ways. There has recently been published a manual in the US of about one hundred and fifty pages of ways to resist taxes. There are some proposals on tactics, too; when the Internal Revenue Services have started seizing people's cars, friends have gone out and bought the cars and given them back. We have had instances when cars were bought for just fractions of a dollar because nobody else wanted to buy a car that was for sale for such reasons. These have become organized events. We have looked at taxes the way we have looked at draft. This is a way of discussing reality, and our response to this institution will make it possible for people (even if they continue paying taxes) to see their lives more imaginatively and to understand the ways in which they have been pushed about. They may not have noticed it, because it's been going on for so long and everybody else is being pushed about like that.

Now as far as the employment question is concerned, we have failed miserably in finding the kind of employment that is really appropriate, but we have been trying very hard. We think that society has a lot of surface needs that are not being met and that people would be happy to help support people who are meeting these needs. It has not been long since teachers were supported not by dollars but by gifts of food and bags of ground wheat to keep going, more a barter/subsistence thing. That is how it goes sometimes. I don't want to give you the impression we are some sort of angels that never get our nails dirty, that we always find ways of winning against Holy Mother the state, we don't, but we are fascinated with the idea of being more peaceful and we believe that we will only be a free and peaceful people when we ourselves as indidividuals are free and peaceful. It's going to come from both directions, but it's not going to come at all if it does not come out of our lives.

Q/C   I would like to raise a question that has not been raised in the whole conference. This is the question of our life-style and support resources in the midst of the consumer society, in your white suburbs, not assuming all the time that it's direct political action of the sort that you have been involved in. I don't belong in that scene at the moment. Nobody is going to ask me to fight in Vietnam. But the danger of being surrounded continually by these white-consumer orientated people and the danger of relapsing back into their life-style and not being a part of it – I thought that this was going to be one of the things this conference was about. I wonder if many people feel that we are not looking at that question hard enough.

J.F.   We generally try to avoid large highly-structured conferences. We came to this one mostly because of friendship with Viv Broughton whom we've known through the years by mail and through the Catonsville Roadrunner. But we have got shy of gatherings anywhere near this big, because the dynamics of the thing are such that it's very difficult to have conversations at any big gathering. It's very difficult to explore generally the kind of question you have raised and the kind of response that would be helpful. I don't want to get in the way a little, just because you are circled around *me*. I'm just as conscious of it as anyone in this room. So ordinarily we flee from these things like the plague. It's just that we believe in the people who have put this together enough to say that this might be an exception. Obviously we hope desperately that out of this will come a lot of contacts in which people will gather to dig much deeper than it is possible to do at something like this.

Q/C   What do you do when you are talking with people who identify with you in your ideas and yet come from a straight background or straight home and have not got the community backing that you have got in your background? One is conscious that one is causing a crack between them and their whole community and I get this all the time talking to schools.

J.F.   One of the gripes I have with the American movement is that it often accentuates this alienation and it does so in a way that is pretty thorough and destructive. There is a story in the gospel about a house-keeper who discovers an evil spirit in the house and gets out a spiritual broom and sweeps the evil spirit out of the house. But what happens? In come seven spirits each more evil than the first. You may say, 'What the hell is that about?' because there is no explanation in the gospel text. I see it as a judgment on the Zealots in Jesus' day – and it's a judgment as well on the movements that I am a part of now. It is easy to describe what is evil in society and to protest and even resist it, but that resistance is absolutely meaningless, in fact worse than meaningless, unless I am involved in helping people to *create* something.

I feel very repentant about the ways in which so many of us in the American resistance communities have not been interested enough in making visible the fact that we are not just resisting. Of course we have to resist. There's no point in allowing the evil spirit to stay there. It's just a matter of dealing with the fact that unless we are putting something in its place, unless we are remaking the house, then we will end up in worse trouble than we were at the start. As regards talking with people, it seems so crucial really to try to be sensitive to what is precious and meaningful to them and to limit the confrontation of ideas to those things that are absolutely essential and of immediate necessity. How easy it is to get waylaid by superficial things that are really tangential. How ironic it is to see how often radicals resemble Christian missionaries who are more the apostles of their particular nationalism, their culture, than of the gospels. The real gospel for the French missionary was French culture. That was the gospel they took to Vietnam. They brought the sacraments of French buildings, French highways, French railway stations, etc., etc. In some places the gospel of Jesus didn't make it.

Q/C   We heard yesterday that we should listen more to the voices of the Third World, and you seem to be speaking very much from the American situation where things are very well organized – where you pay your taxes and you are involved in the war machine. So I just wondered how all this looks to someone from the Third World, and I would like to hear from someone here from the Third World commenting on it.

J.F.   I think for us the people whom we have to try looking at the most are the Vietnamese and the people of Laos and Cambodia. Now the people who have helped us get to that point where we could look at the faces and the bodies of the Indo-Chinese were the blacks, Mexicans and Indians of our own society: America's domestic

Vietnamese. As you probably know, the American peace movement comes directly out of the American civil rights movement. Our communion with Third World people is outrageously faulty, but it's something we are attempting.

I have just come from a second stay in Paris with the Vietnamese Buddhist Peace Delegation. I don't think there is anything that has given us more energy and hope than the Vietnamese and their courage and hope. I have been most especially moved by their non-violent courage which seems to me to be even more remarkable than the violent kind of courage (but every kind of courage moves me). They taught me – without saying a word – that I come from a barbarian and primitive culture that descends from primitive and barbarian cultures. There are few cultures in the world that are yet remotely worthy of the human possibilities. The Vietnamese are one such people.

Q/C   I have been working in the Third World, the Philippines, for the last five years and I came to Huddersfield to find out more about the spiritual dimensions of the liberation struggle. I have been thrilled to be involved in the liberation struggle in the Philippines – a people who for the first time in their history can be conscious of their identity, of their real needs and myself joyfully being privileged to work at their side. Why it is so exciting and what we have to learn, is that it's a non-institutional struggle. We have no model, and even if working out an ideology, we look neither towards Mao nor towards capitalism, we want an ideology that is based on *our* aspirations and hopes as a people. For me, as a priest – I would like to share this with anyone else working in the same position – for me the theology is born of the struggle, and that is why the theology of the Third World is much more vital and dynamic than the theology of the First World. It is being made today, and is born of the struggle. I went there five years ago with no theology and with terrific presumptions that I had some. Thank God I worked with people who were loving enough to help me understand that I knew nothing, but by listening I might pick up something. In the moments of silence that you have mentioned, when I was invited I was able to offer some small insights and experience from my own background. But the experience was merely a learning one and at the side of the people. This Third World theology is so vital because it is happening today with people applying the Christian dimension to the struggle. Communities which arise there are not the institutional communities of Sunday morning churches, but they are born in farmers' movements and in the workers' movements. We have to work so long before liturgies have a place in our struggle, before our celebrations are celebrations of a liberated people. Camilo Torres said this a long time ago. All I can say is that liberation theology is being written *today* in Third World countries, and maybe they have something to offer to people here in the First World. I don't really know, that is why I did not say anything when you spoke. I really don't know – I am Irish and I cannot even understand the Northern Ireland problem. All I can offer is that theology is being written in blood in the Third World, and it's a dynamic theology, and it may be the most authentic theology of today. It's the working people who are writing the theology, because it's merely a reflection on the struggle in the light of Christ. It's a people trying to reflect on themselves, and the norm for Christians is the gospel. I think that is what we have to offer.

J.F.   The only time in my life that I felt that I was really reading the gospels was in prison. The only people in my own society who have been able to make me feel that the Spirit is really breathing down our backs are people who have been in tremendous trouble. I don't mean just in the movement, but those people who are really trying to survive and be alive and to respond to life wherever they may be. It tends to be because they are people on the edge of death. They are people of the Bowery, East Harlem, etc., in tremendous jeopardy all the time. When they talk about anything it seems to me verified in a way that cannot possibly be when I am really speaking out of safety deposit vaults – which is, as you know, where the church has mainly been located these recent centuries. A fact we're trying to change.

PROPERTY
Discussion with Dan Berrigan

Q/C   We are all probably now aware of what *we* can be, but the problem for a lot of us is that in building the alternative there is an element of retreating into self-sustaining communities, which are communities of the spirit, as you have been quite explicit in pointing out. There is an element of retreat in it, the element of saving our own souls, possibly at the expense of wider society. We have got a lot of hope from this conference and may be able to live in these self-sustained communities, but what of people outside, still tied to their cars, holidays abroad, mortgages and so forth? We are looking for help at this point.

D.B.   The supposition in these communities is that every person is anxious to be of service to the community at large. It is very instructive to note that a man like Che Guevara, and some of the heroes of Latin America and some of our domestic heroes as well, have seen themselves in the role of teachers. There is a marvellous passage in the diary of Che, shortly before his death, where he describes how these groups would come into the villages and deal with the people. He said, 'The last thing we ever saw ourselves as was executioners, bloody people, or people who thought they had to kill.' We have found deep resonance there from Vietnamese and among our own people. In our early years these words were unpopular because they were common, near the earth, near to the fact of life; they had so little violence about them. Che goes on to say, 'When we came in we forbade ourselves under the severest penalties, doing anything against the people, even the most recalcitrant landowners.' 'What we tried to do was to gather the people and talk about our lives and that was the revolution.' *And that was the revolution.* It comes like a thump at the bottom of a jump. He goes on to say, 'Though the outside world tried to paint us as bloody killers and as soldiers, as people who had the gun as an extension of their own armed hand, we came in peaceably to teach and to work with the people.'

I don't know how that translates, except that it is our common experience over many years that in every situation including the middle-class, if *you* come unarmed, *they* are disarmed. If you come in without a lot of stereotypes about their sins and your virtues, their cowardice and your heroism, their racism and your purity – if you come in unarmed, as a man or woman of goodwill, you disarm people. There is nothing else to do in face of violence except devise an alternative to it. That takes enormous spiritual resources, because most of us go around armed; it's the ordinary cultural clothing. The society is such that everyone expects at the door either a continual stranger or an active enemy. It comes as a shock that anyone would want to be anything else. That is the way a teacher has to function, to put it crudely, 'I don't have to kill you in order to step over your body to my tomorrow. It is not required. My tomorrow is not that bloody or expedient.'

Q/C   I am glad to be able to agree with Dan Berrigan about finding community around the eucharist. So many of our ideas about community are related to forms of monasticism, where community is defined in terms of property, the house, the land, etc. The early church was very poor and the community was defined by gathering round the eucharist rather than by what they owned.

D.B.   Being in gaol was in many ways like going back to an early monastic experience. We were out of the economy, our rent paid, wearing a common garb, under a common discipline, eating the same food and living the same life day by day. When I came out I would go back there, like the old rabbit who couldn't give up his hole, the former pupil who went back to his old teachers. So I used to go back and visit Philip whenever I got the chance, and see my fellow monks.

But at that time there was a lot of discussion about communities that would buy or rent a house and work out of it, while others would be working apart and come together for sessions. In one town there was a problem about a house and the money for it, and Phil – who, because he was still in prison, had the privilege of getting impatient – said, 'For God's sake, tell them to get out of that dump. If they want to buy something tell them to buy a trailer so they can live while they move, like turtles.' I suppose we need both kinds. The early church found it necessary to live in many places and come together.

Obviously at the deepest level the eucharist was both a mystical bond and a tactical occasion, as we learn from those early letters, letters from prison. We tend to mystify these times, to the point where we lose the practicality of the occasion. I must say that in my chequered career I have never been able to equate my work with my living situation. I guess nobody can these days, really. But it may be helpful to say that the Catholic Worker ideal can be realized in other ways than that of a community living together to do the job.

Q/C   There is something I feel may be of immediate help, and that is that somehow we need to work at finding and living the spirit of poverty. But we need help to understand what it is to find this spirit, to consider our life-styles. To be poor does not mean to be ugly, but to make what we have beautiful but not obscene, and this is very difficult. We have just been given a house, and it is a *fantastic* experience. We have children and we need it, but it does not mean that it is excluded to everyone else. Having these roots is important, but we need help to keep the spirit of poverty.

D.B.   When I hear such a lovely understanding or right attitude to property, it brings me back to that burning scene at Catonsville. We were trying to say of property that unless it is humanly useful and beautiful, it has no right to exist. At the opposite end to what this girl speaks of is this state property. This property symbolizes the will toward death, the power of life and death over people – hunting licences against human beings. There is a kind of schizophrenia, where the property has become the god, so that the oracle is connected with the keepers of the property. At the trial the prosecutor said, 'What you dare to say is that certain properties have no right to exist.' He asked David Harriss, who died later by fire, 'Do you mean that slum properties have no right to exist?' David said, 'Of course they have no right to exist.' He asked for more examples, and David spoke of gas chambers in Nazi Germany, extermination camps and so forth. But equating the draft board with all this was very shattering for Americans: they had never really seen what they were doing. Yet if in local communities there is a very quiet kind of reintegration of property with human life, that is one kind of subtle thinking and appreciation which makes property beautiful, simple and humanly available.

Q/C   What is it about institutions or organizations of human beings that makes them something different from the sum of individuals? I really don't understand what you are talking about. One of the reasons why I say this is because I don't find talk about the devil very helpful either. Somehow I find the devil is really only a projection of things I know to be true about myself. I feel ambivalent towards the

70

state because it is possible to do things with this organization that I cannot do by myself.

D.B. I want to say something about this by returning to the metaphor of the Beast. The Beast was seen as such in the early Christian nightmare because that is the way it appeared in their subconscious. I don't think they meant to say that the state always overtly acts in a bestial way, or that the Beast is never benign. The book is inviting the community to have a certain attitude toward the state. There is a whole complexity of attitudes too, and it makes it very difficult. On the one hand the Christian is indeed commanded to make the revolution. Therefore he has a stake in the state, its form and evolution, its change and betterment. On the other hand, he is commanded to be at the edge of the state, to be a critic, to speak the truth to the state, a truth which in the nature of things is obscure to the state. There are occasions when the Christian submits to imprisonment and indeed death, at the hands of the state. There are other occasions when he can walk hand in hand with the state, in common enterprises, e.g. in the field of social legislation. But, to put it negatively, he never concedes that at its best the state is the kingdom of God, or that the state amounts to the return of the Lord, or the new heaven or the new earth, or any of the other ways the book conceives of the action of God at the end of history. So our attitude towards the state is one of the most active and constant non-violent assault. Right now that is what it involves with us. I don't know a state that does not have prisons, that does not have poor, that does not have international bloody connections especially through money. The trouble with normal times is that the church gets assumed into the whole picture, the good life. The trouble with bad times is that the community gets so isolated from the state that it has nothing really to say to it, nothing to do with it. You may get a country where you can walk with the state – I hope you walk carefully. I hope that the state, however benign, hears from you by way of its unfinished business.

THE EUCHARIST AND SURVIVAL

Discussion with Dan Berrigan

Q/C I would like to follow through on the question of hope. I asked you, Did you see any hope? and you gave what was to me a surprising answer, namely that you saw hope in the gospel, the eucharist and in Christ. I would like you to develop your view on this.

D.B. It does seem to me, and I can only speak about our situation, in the States, that ten years have taught us something at least about the topics that seem to be circulating. I would like to start with a few things about resources, some resources that we have leaned on and tried to draw from and tried to contribute to, because it can't be always just taking without giving something for the future. I want to make a very flat statement about a point of view in this regard, and it's an absolutely absurd statement; it's the statement that 'to be a Christian is of great import'. That is an absurd statement in our culture. To be a Christian is of some import; it's of great import to the community at large; it's of great import to the people who choose to be chosen; it's of great import to the Vietnamese people; it never stops being of import . . . if it is genuine.

The activity, which is at the same time a very deep receptivity, that in some way or other keeps this thing going, is centred upon, in some way, the eucharist and the Bible. We have learned enough to unlearn a lot of theology, and to unravel a lot of very used up and ragged garments that were sort of wrapped around us at birth and don't keep out the cold or the heat or anything else. So we are back really where a lot of people have to begin again, at the beginning. And we have had to understand, and we still do not understand very well, that to read the Bible and to celebrate the eucharist are strictly subversive activities, when they are done correctly. They have nothing to do with inward devotion, except in some accidental way that may be true or not. We don't do them because the country is in a bad state, we do them because we have to do them to exist. But it works, in the country, in the bad state, because it is the right thing to do, the only thing to do. People are always asking us the wrong questions, like 'Why did you go to Catonsville, and how did you weigh things, and what was prison like, and why did you go underground, and why are you so absurd?' But we have to go deeper and begin at the beginning. The beginning is the eucharist-and-the-Bible, which are really hyphenated realities, as you understand. If you want to look upon these things politically, which is to say, in a classic public sense, these actions in bad times are subversive, and according to the Bible the times are always bad just as they are always good. The trouble is, of course, that these things have been done in the wrong way, in the wrong places by the wrong people and so they have been slowly ground into the machinery of non-history which is the history of death, of destruction and of racism and all the things that Colin [Winter] brought up this morning. But when these realities are really isolated by people who are really willing to move with them, something moves. I don't want to say too much about that; I have a very deep sense about it, but like all loving topics, it's also obscure. All of the politics of believers begins with their faith. The symbolic expression of their faith is their willingness to be silent, to listen to the word of God and to break the bread and pass the wine, with all that that implies. 'My body broken for you, my blood given for you.' 'Do this.' We were never really told so clearly to do much else, any more than we were ever told more clearly to stop being political.

The sense of the mystery of life at large and life at small seems to go together, just as for a prisoner on his return to public life all seems to go together, there is no estrangement or derangement or schizo-phrenia. As David Harriss said three years ago, 'When you are on the streets you do that thing; when you are in prison, you do that thing.' You know, keep in going and keep it moving. I don't want to offer proofs for statements that are beyond proof, that is absurd. To say 'this thing works' is the cheapest thing to say about it. The best thing to say about it is that 'we were commanded to do it', and that is our faith. When it is done correctly it gives the community its proper existence; its proper style; its non-violent resources; its proper sexual freedom; its ability to be fruitfully celibate or fruitfully married or fruitfully in love, or whatever you might say; it's compassionate outreach; and perhaps the clearest and the most brutal way of saying it in our country – it's patience with the long haul, in which one does not have to do violence to reach tomorrow, one does not have to step over bodies to create futures. Now from the point of view of the state, all of these attitudes are strictly forbidden, when they are publicly evident. So any gathering that fosters those attitudes and really gets them honest and laid out, and gives people the resources to face them in small groups, and nourishes them, in prison and out, allows them to ride with the horror of life today and to turn it to something compassionate, something even joyful . . . all of that is strictly anti-state activity, because it leads to Catonsville, or Milwaukee with Jim, or a hundred other centres where you are in trouble; it sets a clear path. Suppose that during the eucharist, as always happens, the scripture is being read and meditated on, and people are rational and clear and together about where they are going, because they have heard this or that word, about where to go (scripture is not about outer space, it's about where to go). I say that the combination from the state's point of view is lethal, and from our point of view, is life-giving. I don't want to make any of these statements a kind of judg-ment about other people who start from other points of view. I am talking about us, presumably, what we have found. The worst thing we could do in prison, from the point of view of the prison, was to celebrate the eucharist and read the scripture. It held us together, it kept us ready, it kept us hopeful, it got us prepared for this, for coming out again, and it formed a community in there that did not give up, did not give up, and is now together in New York where things are worse than ever. It introduced a common discipline, and connected us with a common tradition, and God knows we have been saying for fifteen years in the States, 'If you are trying to go somewhere and don't come from somewhere, you are lost.'

Q/C   You are talking about the tradition, and leading into that tradition, but is it not arguable that the tradition of which you your-self are a part, the celebration of the mass, and the priesthood and the Catholic church, has, next to the state, been the major instrument of oppression in the world?

D.B.   I haven't been! I am not talking about the Catholic church as such, understood as incorporating Cardinal Spellman. I am talking about a few Christians who are trying to find a way in their tradition. I don't want to be cold about it, but your question is irrelevant. Yes, yes, the answer to your question is Yes, but it's irrelevant. I am not Cardinal Spellman.

Q/C   I don't think it's too irrelevant, Dan. One thing that bothers me is why the gospel, and why Christianity can produce and has produced historically, such a corrupt structure, such a corrupt church. This whole question of the label Christianity is very much a problem for me, I can no longer consider myself a Christian in any sense of the word, except historically. I think this whole question of why the gospel is one thing to you and is something else to another person, is very relevant.

D.B.   I guess we can debate that. I don't think that was what we began with. No. Why don't you go ahead if you want to? I don't know too much about it, because I have never been in that church.

Q/C   But that is avoiding the issue, because you were in fact talking about belonging to a tradition and we are not talking about you, we are talking about your tradition, and what it is in that tradition that you find so attractive when to so many people that tradition has a whole history of oppression, etc., etc.

D.B.   What do I find so attractive? What I tried to talk about, prayer and scripture and the eucharist.

JIM FOREST   I would just like to throw a saying in that I find helpful. It's from a Quaker source. 'When the devil takes the camp, he seldom bothers to change the flag.'

Q/C   (African) There are three questions here that I feel are open to provide a guideway; the eucharist, your philosophical way and the way you understand it; I don't think the audience sitting down here is benefiting in the way in which they want to hear from you. On the other hand, can you tell us, what role does tradition play in our lives as Christians today, and should we, in this age, still abide to this tradition? This is what this young man wants to know from those of us who read the Bible, because if we talk in the way we understand according to our traditions we still keep them confused and they don't know where they belong. Now let us come out and speak the truth as Jesus wants us to speak it. I belong to a tradition, but I tell you something here, that I don't see the place of that tradition in my Christian life. And I don't practise it, because I see that tradition does not have any longer have any place in the passing of the message to those who need it today.

D.B.   Maybe it would be helpful to say what I mean by a tradition. I was suggesting, in a very clumsy way, the links that bind a believing community today to a community of believers at the time the gospels were written. The inner freedom to by-pass all the tremendous sins and derangements and crimes of the time between, and that is the connection that I think important, to do those things laid out for us in the gospel and to live according to that style.

Q/C   (*Children of God*) As far as I can see, by just trying to abide in the traditions you are just going to perpetuate them, and if you continue in any way to try and change traditions by going along with part of them, you will find that in the end you will be going along with all of them. The way Jesus had to do it was to step out of the religious establishment and actually just show them up for what they were. He did not do that just by preaching it, so much as actually by doing it. I don't know whether we will change things by just having a eucharist, maybe a change of format in eucharist. We need a complete change of heart in our whole way of life.

D.B.   The eucharist is a whole way of life.

Q/C   Is there not some confusion there between tradition and traditions? If you call yourself a Christian and you read the Bible, immediately you are dealing with tradition, something which happened in the past and you are keeping links with it. If you want to drop the Bible, drop Christianity, that way you drop tradition completely. But that seems to me to be the essential message and the actual tradition as opposed to traditions.

Q/C   I thought the idea was to have a kind of dialogue with Dan and with other people, because I personally dislike the idea of the guru-type relationship which I think it is very easy to get into, if you have one person who alone is allowed to speak, and utters forth words of wisdom. I would much prefer to have dialogue in which we can say 'you are talking nonsense' if that is what we feel he is talking, and he can say it back to us.

Q/C   One of the dilemmas of a lot of people who have come here is that the so-called radical Christian movement in this country, emanating I suppose from your initial action, has been going four or five years. We have left the church, basically, in an established sense. I think a lot of us are struggling to know whether we ought to resurrect another one or build an alternative. What do we do with tradition, with worship, with this whole thing which we call spirituality really, and which a lot of us cannot even define? I am not asking you to comment on that necessarily; I am just trying to voice perhaps what other people feel. Is that what people feel? Have you left the church? Is the debate about whether we work inside the church or outside the church? Is that debate still valid? Because I think the assumption behind this conference is that it is no longer valid, it is a dead issue.

Q/C   I think it's easy for Dan Berrigan because he is a priest and can celebrate the eucharist. Can I celebrate the eucharist, or do I need you or someone like you?

D.B.   In our tradition the priest is required. I think there are all kinds of traditions and we do all kinds of eucharist, depending on the assembly. When Philip got out of prison on 20 December, hundreds of people came to the prison and we had a eucharist, and it included Jews and all kinds of people. We improvised the blessing over the bread and wine, to try to express the occasion, you know what I mean. Something that would not be offensive to, let's say Buddhists, and Jews and all kinds of people.

Q/C   I can get along with the gospel of Christ but I am a bit worried about the eucharist. It seems to me that I can have the eucharist, too, but have I got to have somebody, a priest, in order to have it?

D.B.   This is our community belief, within the Catholics. This is the way we celebrate. If we have Quakers present or others present then we try to be faithful to that occasion, and do it the way everyone would like.

Q/C   There is, of course, in the Bible the priesthood of all believers. I have myself in Africa, just as an ordinary steward, broken bread with members of the congregation. The nearest church is fifty miles away, and the person is dying. By the time the priest gets there he will be dead, so I break the bread and give him wine, and we have a meal, and I am quite sure – I *know* – that the person dying during the night, died happily, and nobody has ever questioned my right to do it. God called me to share in this kind of meal with the bread and wine, with this soul before she died, and she departed and went *straight to heaven*. I assure you I have seen it.

Q/C   As far as I can see, you are trying to break out of the traditional whole of the church and get more freedom of expression; and in some ways you make out that the main emphasis is political. Am I right in saying that?

D.B.   Yes. Another way of saying it is that we are trying maybe to grope our way back to the real tradition which is political. Worship is political, and real politics is worshipful.

Q/C   Can I just make the point that the same Jesus who says, 'Go and teach all nations,' is the one who says, 'Without me you can do nothing.' I would say that surely the theological idea behind the eucharist is that in a community, a small community, you unite yourself with Christ, working on the principle that before you love 'everyone' you must love someone somewhere. And then you go out and extend that, you don't stop there.

Q/C   But I don't understand what that means, this magic bit about Jesus and the eucharist. I can understand what you say, that a particular ritual or a particular part of the gospel you get involved in or meditate or concentrate on, can mean something. But I don't understand this idea of Jesus popping out of a hat all the time.

Q/C   I think the biggest insight I had about the eucharist was when I attended a communion in the United Reformed Church. Before the communion they read the passage about the road to Emmaus when the disciples did not know Jesus after the resurrection until he broke bread with them, and immediately they recognized them. To follow on this tradition, I think, gives the biggest insight. If you share a meal with someone, you know them. If you sit opposite someone at a table at the conference you converse with them during the meal. You get to know them. And I think it is an analogy with that.

D.B.   I think we are all troubled with this connection that we are groping towards. It is really something that's so simple it is very hard to get at. I thought some of the expressions used were very interesting, e.g. the idea that from a scripture text Jesus pops out of a hat or something. With that we are right back into old magic, or decadent Catholicism. That's just the kind of thing we are leaving behind us, really. Again, I don't want to give the impression that I am trying to prove anything – I think that would be very bad – but to share certain experiences that have been very difficult and very fruitful for us. When we were arrested they took us to this county gaol for a week and we fasted and waited developments. Then one of our friends got us in some bread and wine one day, and we said to the warden (because we didn't want to fool around in a corner), that we wanted to have religious observance. He was a very amazing guy and he said, 'You mean a eucharist?' and we said 'Yeah,' and he said 'You can have it if I can come.' It was very amazing, this guy was so troubled and so touched by the people he had to keep under lock and key. He was a Catholic and he said that he wanted to be there. So we went ahead and had that. These are very deep waters and very hard to express.

Then the morning we went on trial, which was a month later, we said to him again that we wanted to have a eucharist, and he said

'Fine,' and we did. That's the way we went to trial. It is like that pause before you go on to another task. When we went then two years later into the Federal prison for our real sentence, that still lingered as the thing to do at times, not regularly, not on schedule – at times. Occasions, such as in prison, would call for it. When a friend was being plucked out or transferred and put in chains, or when one of us was leaving . . . you tried to follow the rhythm of the place. But you did need that pause, and I don't know how to put it except to say that prison is so deranging, it is even more deranging than the world, more damaging to people's skulls, that at times you really have to call a halt and listen for a while, and do something that allows you to regain your consciousness, and to admit who you are with one another. There are all sorts of ways of putting it. So we were trying to break free from the damaging routine of prison, as we are trying to break free of the damaging and killing routine of the world, by going to Catonsville and breaking the law, to break free from the routine of war, so we can still continue this. It seemed to mean something to all kinds of people, to all kinds of prisoners who were in our circle for various kinds of reasons, who were wrestling with their own lives, who had come to prison for these absurd little crimes against money and cars and all that, and yet were becoming very aware politically. These things went on, and we came out gradually. Philip and the others were still on trial when I came out a year ago. Harrisburg was in full swing and down there we did the same thing. Several of the prisoners joined us, ex-prisoners, to work at the trial, and then we all got our land legs in our own town in New York, and decided where we were going, which is to stay there, because ex-prisoners could meet and work there, and we did the same thing, you know, just kind of part of the rhythm of things. I am sure that other people have other ways of resisting the collective insanity which goes by the public name of 'law and order'. This was one of our ways.

I am sure other people have very different ways of dealing with the deep violence which is in their bones, and which the culture just tries desperately to keep going again. So that you have to be constantly purifying youself of that mirror image of the enemy which leads you to pick up guns because the mirror has a gun. So, to work at your life, which is the beginning of the movement, to work at your lives together, which is the continuation of the movement, all these things: we found it very necessary to confess our violence or hatred, our fear, our dread of life, our itch towards death . . . all the things by which we are condemned to be Americans, as you are condemned to be yourselves. We found at least that this was a help, to give ourselves time to breathe and to create space around us where the culture would grant us nothing, and to admit something of transcendence in our lives, where the culture would flatten us out with its steam-roller. It was opposition, it was resistance all the way to do these things. And it kept us going. We are among very few survivors of the sixties; there are not many of us left. Some of us in our minds visit the grave-yard of companions all the time. People who have declared themselves dead to us, dead to movement, dead to hope, dead to compassion. That's all I have to share with you, you know. There is something about endurance that needs more than a culture, unless your endur-ance is built on money and pride and the death of others. So in order to stay out of that movie* last night (which was at one point night-mare and at another point illusion, and was not very helpful about our scene), to stay out of that movie, which is another point of view, essentially an American movie, to stay out of that bloodshed, we needed something, and this was the way we found it, it's the way we are still finding it. We are still on our feet. We have been through more than nine-tenths of the people who began with us in the sixties, not to speak of the mass of our people. We're still going and we're still hopeful and we're still sane, sort of. I'm trying to share with you some of the ingredients of whatever it is.

Q/C   What makes people leave? You say you have been through people and you have visited the graveyards: do you mean people who have succumbed to the middle-class, to the pressures of society?

D.B.   It's too long, it's too hard, it's too demanding, it's too ridden with illusions, it's too rhetorical. 'People forgot,' as Camus said in his novel, 'People forgot to be modest.'

Q/C   May I ask you why you are a Jesuit?

D.B.   Many in the Order would deny your statement. Well, I find it very interesting. There are some very nice, very good people. For the first time in my life I am involved in a classroom situation with young Jesuits this year at the seminary there in New York, and I find, yeah, it's not bad. We have an ecumenical thing going now, with the Protestant faculty, and so we meet a very wide variety of students from all over the country. It's like saying, 'Why are you happily married?' The question brings you up short. If you are happily married you don't think about it too much.

Q/C   What motivates the younger generation of Jesuits at the moment?

* Punishment Park.

80

D.B.   I think they are very highly motivated by their sense of obscurity. They are willing to enter into a classroom situation where people are, I think, trying to find a way together, and especially having a Protestant seminary nearby is very important and very fruitful, and sheds a lot of light in a lot of directions. I hesitate to say that obscurity is ever unlimited; I think that obscurity is limited by our own lack of imagination and all, but pooling things gets us a little further. You see, we are really in a situation where we could say a few things about our seminaries. Number one, they are all coming down. That's the first good news. Number two, practically nobody knows they are all coming down. Number three, people as a consequence of number two are acting as though they are not coming down. I have often been in the country where they have pools that dry up in the course of the summer. On the surface you have life going on, bugs, leapfroggers and all, and they don't really know that the whole thing is drying up, and at the end of the summer they are in trouble. Number four, somebody had better be thinking of alternatives, so that is what we are trying to do. Meantime we use the seminary as a way of getting something real going, while it comes down. It has been said, 'You build something new and it shall be the old.'

Q/C   We have an alternative which many people disagree with but which I think is the only way we can do it, and that is by following Jesus' direct example. There are many people in the churches who just don't want to be changed. But that is the way to change, just to go on doing what you know to be best, and what I know to be best is to follow Jesus. And inevitably, if anyone lives the life of Christ, or gets as near to it as possible, that will cause a fantastic change, and revolution will be inevitable. Communities of the Children of God have sprung up all over the place, in about three years. From a group of friendly people in California, it is now in or about forty countries in the world, and multiplying really fast. Not so much in numbers but just in impact. It is not just to say that we are a numerous body particularly, but the impact of what we are doing is having an effect upon the world, quite outstanding in some ways. We are not wanting to brag too much about the Children of God, but just to say that this is what happens when you decide to pay heed to God's word.

Q/C   I would like to add to that something that Samson cannot say. I know the man who has just spoken and I have lived in Notting Hill for the last ten years, the equivalent of East Harlem. I know that this Christmas Day and this Boxing Day all the social workers in Notting

Hill and all the ministers in Notting Hill, like me, were gathered around our own fires, having a very nice time with our families, and the only people on the streets who were looking after the 250 youngsters, many of whom are taking narcotics, and sleeping in doorways and abandoned cars, the only people doing a great *celebration* in terms of dancing and singing and loving and giving them roast lamb, which they were roasting on a charcoal fire, were Samson and people like him, the Children of God. This is a judgment on me as a churchman, and a judgment on the Catholics and Anglicans and all the rest of it in my situation.

JIM FOREST Visit with Buddhists in Vietnam. I continued to think during the course of these discussions, that there has been a certain kind of theological imperialism, or Christian chauvinism, that does not make much room for the dignity of other religious traditions. I just wonder if you could comment at all on the possibility that there is a kind of Christian chauvinism that is at work in the Christian world, that leaves us deaf and blind to other religious traditions.

D.B. Jim brought up a question of our relationship with the Vietnamese Buddhists which really goes back several years now, and I would just like to share some precious high points in all that. I think they shed light in our direction. I think it was in 1965 that Thich Nhat Hanh first came to the States and really was our first experience, up close, of any kind of Buddhist tradition, particularly of a Buddhist monk. He subsequently went down to visit with Thomas Merton and they spent several days together. In the course of their visit they made a tape, and sent it to me, and that became one of our lost treasures. We never found out what happened to this tape later. They discussed the kind of meeting point between their experiences as Western monk and Eastern monk, and sang to one another, Gregorian chant and Buddhist chant, and compared them, and talked very deeply about a lot of things. Merton was beginning, even then, to get into very hot water for his writings on racism and nuclear arms and Cold War; he saw a lot of this coming. What really struck me was that both of these monks were meeting as very worldly people in a special way. Nhat Hanh had been thrown out of Vietnam because he had become very dangerous, very hot, because he was leading the church and young people in a direction that the government was getting quite annoyed at. So I think that was a new realm. We had always realized that in Buddhism there was a contemplative tradition, but we had never realized that there was an immense kind of moral and social passion functioning. Thich Nhat Hanh had already found it and was leading the school for social action in Saigon, training young people to go into the villages and do all kinds of work with people, teaching, rehabilitation, farming and all the rest of it. This was a work that was very unpopular, as you can understand, with a regime that wanted to control everyone and everything, and wanted the religion to be in its own service, etc. Anyway, he came out and he could not get back, and providentially became our friend. He came to Paris later and established there the Buddhist church delegation to the talks and they got under way, and he has been in Paris pretty much ever since.

This insight has come to me since visiting him in Paris again and spending time with the Buddhists. The Buddhist's church is in a position *vis-à-vis* the children of Saigon which is almost exactly opposite to the position of the Catholic church and the Christian church *vis-à-vis* Nixon in the States. It's a tremendous bloodstained irony that is operating here, because Nhat Hanh is one of the most respected Buddhists in the world, and within his own church is leading a non-violent revolution in his own country that is placing a gauntlet between the survival tactics of the North and the Vietcong on the one hand and the tyranny of Thieu and the Americans on the other, whereas in the States there has been almost complete capitulation to the culture, to the violence, to the war, by the church officially speaking. So talk about having something to learn, I guess that is what I am trying to say, talk about having something to learn. Because we, as clumsy members of a rather long resistance group, have realized that here is a church that is acting as perhaps Jesus envisioned the Christian church to act. That is to say, to be in perpetual friction and conflict with the state on questions of human life, on questions of survival, on questions of defence of the poor and the innocent, and the victimized. So there we are with a bad network of social and charitable and reconstruction projects which, as I say, are acts of non-violent resistance, which so permeate the culture, and so permeate the society, that there is nothing to do with these people; they have locked up thousands of them, created new tiger cages for them. Sweep them into the armed forces, violating all Vietnamese traditions, e.g. monks now are supposed to fight, or, lower the age of military induction so that you can grab novices out of the Buddhist pagodas for the army. If Nhat Hanh were here he could do this very much better than any of us.

I have to say to you very frankly that many of the things that our young people in the West are either blind to in their own tradition, or angrily rejecting in their own religious tradition, are exactly the things that constitute Buddhist resistance. That is the irony for us, that we cannot really dig in and find out a tradition that will help us be recognizable and resisting people in our culture, and the Vietnamese and the Buddhists have never lost this thing, never lost it. They talk, as I have tried to talk, about their life of worship and their life of prayer, and then very naturally of their life of resistance as one life, as one life. If it is true that one of the elements that is keeping together a very assaulted, death-threatened country, as Vietnam, is keeping it miraculously together and alive after all these years, it is certainly the Buddhist story. That has something to say to us, of a tradition that has its roots in meditation and worship and celibacy and service, public service, and therefore has been able, as one of the chief elements, to keep the country alive when the US had decreed that it should die, and it has not died. I have certainly talked to some knowledgable Americans who have been over there and in very difficult long-term circumstances, who believe that the Buddhists, together with other elements, have shifted the whole centre of civilization as far as the future goes, by their willingness to encounter the machine as human beings; to confront it non-violently; to stay alive, and to say something that we ourselves are too scared to say, that is, that man is greater than the machine. Because most of us practically no longer believe it, which is one way of putting our despair. In that little broken country we have all the ironies of the New and the Old Testament functioning, the remnant, with regard to the despised remnant of the Third World, that meets the Beast, and turns it back. Some day, when all the headlines have been written, and we begin the search for the truth, the Buddhist story will be a very precious element. Some of us have already been nourished by it, very deeply. We really believe that without a religious non-violent tradition functioning in the modern state, nothing is going to get very far, and we are really kind of gladly arrogant about it, and about keeping this thing going.

Q/C Do you regard the non-violent teaching, etc., as centring on the same deity, or do you regard them as devices merely for maintaining this humanistic tradition?

D.B. I really would not want to look on anything human as a device for anything else, otherwise we are really defining a machinery rather than a human community. I think that people are religious probably because that is a very precious and ancient way of being human, and that is a value to itself. The fact that it is useful or useless in history is quite secondary. Of course the fact is that it is always useful when it is itself, but that is very secondary. It is there, and when it is genuine it is there, and when it is not genuine it is poisonous, it is another element in the machinery of death which is the rolling on of history, history being that which is always written by the winners about the losers.

I have felt for a long time that we and the West are progressively giving up on any recognizable definition of human beings, and that our imagination is constantly being plucked over to the point where we are really accepting machinery and the machine as our future. And so metaphors about efficiency and movement and results and devices and tactics and all that, is all the triumph of the machine, the invasion of the human being by the machinery and the levelling off of the human community into another element of the machine. Five years ago they told us that in the making of computers human beings are defined as 'bio-chemical links'. They are certain, temporary, faulty links between two machines, which will some day shortly be dispensed with. We won't need bio-chemical links, because we will have machines supplying their own links. Meantime, of course, it is really very difficult to recognize that human life and love and community, a lot of very despised but beautiful truthful things, had nothing to do with anything around us except ourselves. Whether or not they work, is a profoundly anti-human, possibly pagan, view. If we ever in our lifetime had the fortune to meet a saintly Buddhist or a saintly Christian, I feel quite sure he would have a very different vocabulary from ourselves and our movement, a very different vision of the world. The last thing on his horizon would be whether or not his life was 'working', because he probably would be on welfare, and so his life would not be 'working'.

Q/C   Could you say whether Pentecostalism has a positive role, or whether or not it is an escape from the real issues?

D.B.   It is very hard for me to speak on. I know a lot of people who are into it; I have never been able to connect with it myself. What we saw of it in gaol among certain young prisoners was usually in connection with the drug culture or connected with the people who were into Zen Buddhism or something like that, but it was very difficult for us to establish connections of concern with people like that. Our feeling was that practically every movement (this was part of the high wire act, I think, that we were trying to put on, that the consciousness in our country is so disintegrated), that practically every movement turns out very shortly to be a middle class luxury and another way of getting away from the horror of what is happening, whether it is Esalen, or Skinner, or a lot of the new religious movements. Their master image is not the rhythms of the world but it's the drug culture, it's another drug, it's a way of forgetting the unbearable facts of what's happening. So you have to be able to give it a good name like 'charismatic renewal' in order to mask the fact that people don't want to leave the house, because there is blood on the streets.

Q/C Do you have a concept of God?

D.B. A concept of God? Not really, if I had one I would certainly get rid of it quickly. We used to call it temptation.

Q/C Do you have a way of defining the term God?

D.B. I don't like defining the term, because I don't think he is a term. I like to read the New Testament and I get along with that.

Q/C I think that this is a very important question he is touching on, in looking for a concept of God, particularly in relation to the problem of communication. I work in a very secular culture, and the type of people that I have been working with and trying to relate to are people like International Socialists, or the Communist societies, and this has been very difficult because they have not been brought up in a Christian culture and do not understand the language. It is a particular problem in relation to motivation, how to keep their struggle and our struggle going. We are now lacking in motivation at this point. What is it we want to do in the new society? What the hell are we fighting for, anyway? Why should I bother? We have used Christianity for so long to try to get a new sense of motivation. Okay, I have failed to communicate something of what Christianity means. We don't want to encapsulate God, but we need some sort of level of communication with people in a secular culture. When we were planning this thing at the beginning, we had the subtitle 'Spiritual dimensions to political struggle'. So far I feel there has been very little appreciation of this central question that we had in mind. Too much has been taken for granted.

D.B. Yes, you are right. You see, I can only admit to very severe limitations in regard to what you bring up because I guess there is no more secular mix in the world than the one we are trying to deal with. At least, I haven't seen one. We have found by a lot of trial and error and blood and sweat that the best thing we could do to communicate in or to exist in, or whatever you try to do in this secular culture, was to return to our roots and try to be faithful to them. And strangely enough we found that when we did that we did the best thing we could for our culture, because we were really saving it from itself. And we won the admiration of our culture because we did a lot of things that people in the culture were afraid to do, like break the law and go to gaol, though the war was everybody's burden. So it is really very strange. I think that if I ever had periods when I betrayed what was best in what I should do, it was when I tried to get away from all this, and to meet that thing on its own grounds, and to forget where I came from, and the time when I was closest to all kinds of people, whether in gaol or New York City, was when they were interested that there was someone taking the Bible seriously. Then we can begin to talk.

Now you know I am surrounded by faculty members who are experts in Christianity, far ahead of myself, and very few of whom are Christians. They lead the students down that same alley – experts always produce experts, it's a computer law – and they go around very happy because they are making the culture, they are very interested in psychology and counselling and group dynamics and sociology, and very few of them have any practical juices to offer anyone in theology and in scripture. And very few of them ever say a word about the war, and very few of them have ever been seriously disturbed about anything. So my theory is that that kind of meeting between so-called culture and so-called religion is helping the culture go deeper into its death game and encouraging it in the conviction that religion has nothing to offer. In our culture we have never met anyone who shared our social concerns who was not passionately interested in our religion.

Q/C To what extent are your life-style and your actions based on your experience of God or your interpretation of the Bible?

D.B. I don't know how to say 'to what extent'. It seems to me to be one thing. I really have never experienced God, I have tried to believe in him. I can't conceive of myself not believing, I guess that is a great gift too. I don't know where I would go if I did not believe. I guess that would be despair or exile or somewhere.

Q/C Dan, when you say that you do not experience God, but you believe in him, I think this kind of phrase could be scandalous, because a lot of us feel that we do experience God, but we experience God only through men the whole time. You know, people look upon this as their belief, and therefore they say, 'I do experience God, but not in an interventionist sense.'

Q/C I would like to say that in my experience the only kind of mystery there is in life is in other people. The old traditional thing is that God is a mystery you can never fathom, but you know it is in other people you meet. You can't pigeonhole them either, they are in a sense an infinite mystery. Insofar as you get into that kind of mystery, you are getting near to what people have always meant by 'God'. Apart from that there is very little meaning in the word God.

D.B.   I get a little uneasy with the kind of view that reduces the experience of God to one's neighbour. I think that is a very important aspect, but I don't think it is everything.

Q/C   What place do you see for the contemplative life, in view of this relationship of God and other people?

D.B.   It is very interesting that a man like Thomas Merton hung around a monastery all his adult life, and he was very very conscious of the irony and absurdity of it all, and often expressed that. I think in a sense he almost hung around because it was absurd, because he was a very modern kind of man in that way. So he used to say that he would certainly never become a monk again if he had to do it over, but that he was not about to leave since he had done it. I think there is a lot of very nice stuff in there somewhere. The young people across the country are beginning to discover Merton all over again because maybe they have gone through this kind of enormous tunnel of the sixties and see the deadly quality of trying to create alternatives that have no inside to them, that are pure 'outside' like the culture itself, pure 'give away'. They are finding in him a tremendous range of understanding and depth that he could have spoken about the Cold War and the Hot War and the nuclear build-up and the racial crisis before they happened because he had a kind of extra-sensory apparatus functioning through his prayer, through his reading and pondering. Maybe he is going to help us get to a better balance of things, that we don't have to freak out in order to have an interior, and we don't have to turn ourselves inside out in a cultural sense either. We can have both which is a good definition of sanity, maybe.

Q/C   Wasn't Merton very conscious of these problems outside the monastery, yet he had a great urge to be a hermit?

D.B.   Of course, he did live as a hermit in his last years. What he was really thwarted in was his dream, which was about ten years old at the time of his death. It was to establish a kind of new hermitage. He wanted very much to go to Latin American and establish, in the slum areas, a little group of contemplatives, maybe two others and himself, and maybe just let things happen from there. He was never allowed to do that. But the very fact that one speaks of a man like that, as not being allowed to do something, is one way of putting the mystery, that he submitted. The fact is that he could have walked out and done it anytime he wanted to, but he wouldn't because he was a monk. While ninety per cent of our people were tearing themselves apart in the frenzies of the sixties, he was telling us what it was all about. In a very nice, indirect, non-exhorting way, he was showing us a way. We are just beginning to see it.

Q/C   Can I ask you whether, knowing what you know now, and having been through what you have been through, you would still become a priest?

D.B.   I never even think of it, but I guess so. Certainly it has never been dull.

Q/C   Dan, would you like to say something about Jesus as the outsider, who is the great enabling exemplar for our times?

D.B.   I can remember that the first time we went down to visit Merton we started talking about the monk as the outsider, which was very strange because he was so very far inside, but that was not spiritual with him, that he was inside, because he was always at the edge, not exactly outside, but at the edge. I think this is an even richer term because you can move in either direction, and constantly do. You are moving with those who are out and those who are in and those who are passing both ways, and can speak that kind of language to people who are in very severe quandaries about their lives. He was the kind of person who always could have taken the corrupt benefits of the establishment of the church or the state, could have become a kind of monk celebrity, but he always kept lean and kind of angry and kept an edge to himself, kept bringing up unpleasant things, kept getting into trouble. That was very important, you know, because part of the cultural thing within the church too is that if you get a reputation you are supposed to make a gentlemen's agreement, which goes like this: 'We will agree, those of you who admire me and I who admire you because you admire me, we will both agree that the issues for which you got to admire me are going to be gradually submerged in your admiration of me.' So what really comes about after a while, with most of these figures, is that you pass from a person who is really sharp and prophetic about issues into someone who is at the bad centre of things being admired. The day in which the culture can help you forget the death of a Vietnamese because you have been made into a media-freak or a celebrity, they've won again. This was very rough when I came out of gaol. I understood it all over again, how the whole thing was to devour you to the point where they could build a statue of you, instead of remaining with the issues that got you in trouble, and for which you should be in trouble, as long as you live.

I didn't want to get into all that, except that with Merton it was a very clear monk's calling to him, to be in trouble about the right things at the right time. They never won over that; he died that way. It was very good, very good for all of us.

Q/C   How did he die?

JIM FOREST   He was an anti-technologist who collided with technology. An electric fan fell on him and the electric shock caused a heart attack and killed him.

D.B.   I have to tell a little story in this regard. You know the 'Merton-thing' has got many amazing things around it. We are still sorting them out. John Howard-Griffin, who is crippled, so he was in a wheelchair, was down living in the cabin after Merton died, living in the sort of hut where he had lived. He was writing, taking notes of all this stuff, writing Merton's biography. One night while he was working there was a tremendous storm over the mountains, and things got nearer and nearer, and finally the cabin was struck by lightning and the lightning came down the chimney or something and struck the metal wheelchair that he was in and knocked him across the room. He was thinking of the way Merton had died and that it was probably dangerous to pick the pieces up. So don't get too close to Merton!

Q/C   Dan, I'd like to bring you back to the eucharist you were talking about. How do you approach the eucharist, as it were, insofar as we who are traditional Christians, approach the eucharist and look on it really in a magical sort of way? And what about de Chardin, the very deep sense of the spiritual that he got from the eucharist? What is your experience from the eucharist?

D.B.   To us, it's sort of survival, and very few of us can read Chardin any more about anything because of what we went through. It seems to us that he was very good about the end out there, but we are trying to take the next step. I don't know how to put it, except that it seems to have a deep rightness, that we do this in obedience to a tradition and that the accompanying reading and meditation on the scripture helps us to go on.

PART THREE

Will there be a Harvest?

Viv Broughton
RISKS OF LIBERATION

For me it was all pure paradox, We had spent the best part of a life-time trying to make sense of a world that seemed to have a compulsive need to eat its young, and now it seemed we would turn right around and begin to make a nonsense out of it. For a long time we had under-stood that oppression is to be dealt with by the way of all flesh (up and at 'em) and here we were, punch-drunk freedom fighters, spending a few days seeking God or truth or even . . .

Back in the balmy days of 1968, Rev. James Bevel put it this way: 'We've got to get left of Marx, we've got to get left of Lenin, we've got to get right on out there up on that cross with Jesus.' Well, it was 1968, but even now we were in no mood for mere frivolity and still less were we in the mood for mere theology or politics. Perhaps it was true that most of the clues to some kind of redeemed future lay in the terri-tory beyond the first turning on the left. It was equally true that this was occupied territory for the most part, and that having come upon its border guards we had (for the most part) turned and fled. It is said that churchwardens were surprised by their own strength. Now, we have been frozen in our tracks at the discovery that in retreat, our style of operation has been defined in almost every respect by the style of the enemy – so much so that you could almost say we faced a mirror image of all that had disallowed the revolution. Paradoxically, the movement for liberation has been weakened in direct proportion to its strength and military potency and its ostensible ability to 'deal a body blow to capitalism'. We are staggered, I'm sure, to discover that all these truths we held to be self-evident are nothing more than illusion, but it is one of the obscure jokes of the Christian gospel that we are all required to stand on our heads from time to time.

Nobody, as far as I know, laid aside a gun to make the journey to Huddersfield, but there were many of us there who are up to our eyes in grass-roots agitation for social and political change. Mostly I guess, we had seen radical political action as an expression of our inherited

Christian faith, until one by one we came to the awful realization that the deed and its propaganda were all. There was no God that we knew of, only analysis and practice; and now even the practice (upon analysis) proved to be dying at the heart. Like so many before us, it seemed that we too would prove to be damp squibs with a short burn of bright light before an anti-climatic retirement. Either that or infuse our politics with the same frustration and bitterness and defeat that have for ever been corpuscles in the life-blood of statesmen. *Either way we would soon become the enemy.*

But, and here is another paradox, there is just the faintest chance that if we are prepared to so risk our spiritual defeat, we may also chance upon a real liberation of the spirit. Certainly the former is a precondition of the latter, and the latter, in the end, is all that matters. In the end, what we seek as an alternative to involuntary poverty is not riches, but life and the means and will to celebrate that life. So we came to Huddersfield, many of us, because the suspicion persisted that somewhere buried deep beneath bestiality posturing as religion, might lie the one clue by which we might begin to unravel the primary paradox that undermined our every day: that life, to be celebrated to the full, must be fully discarded. And all our attempts to advance the quality of our life and all the defences we put up to safeguard it, are entirely counter-productive (if 'productivity' had any meaning in this context).

It is for this reason that we must take seriously Chris Duncan's charge that to talk of liberation and revolution without talking about class struggle, is to create yet one more mystification. To be more specific, the overwhelming majority at Huddersfield were carrying with them the mark of class privilege, the tickets and documents that allow one to lead a fully productive life in society. And you can be sure that in this context, 'productivity' does have meaning. We have yet to see any serious refusal of tickets and documents, or any serious rejection of the many and subtle privileges of middle-class breeding. The mark of the Beast for us is privilege, and we all wear the mark, even though reluctantly at times. It must therefore be an absolute pre-condition of all else we do, that we extricate ourselves from the community that exists by the subjugation of others, and consciously opt to be part of a community whose very survival is daily threatened. Only then can we legitimately speak of creating and celebrating life while surrounded by a poverty of spirit. This paradox at least is consistent.

> We Christians are like seeds
> and the people are like the soil.
> Wherever we go we must
> united with the people,

take root
and blossom among them.   *Mao Tze Tung S.J.*

Our four-day communion – what else can I call it – was so exhaustingly
ecstatic that the aftermath must be subjected to the most rigorous
examination; not a cold dissection of a distinctly sweaty experience,
but a time for greater honesty as a result of our days together. If it was
not all wind and piss, as they say in that part of Yorkshire, was it all
fun and games, a great party? A loaded question, of course, with the
dour implication that fun and games are of no consequence, but we
began with an affirmation that true spirituality is inextricably bound
up with the harshest political reality. That, for me, is as true in euphoria
as it is in defeat and I must be rude and ask: despite our determination
to retain a hold on reality, are we simply developing a new and more
enticing distraction? Are we in any way better equipped to deal with
internal and external enemies as a result? Has anything changed in the
ghettoes of these islands or is it still business as usual?

For those of us who in most circumstances would wish to be known
as political agitators, but in certain special circumstances might risk the
mark of Christ, there is one question concerning the revolutionary
struggle that we alone will be disposed to face and which might make
all the difference: what is the paradoxical relationship between faith
and action, or if you prefer, between the spiritual and the political? On
all the evidence amassed over the centuries of thought and experience,
they are absolutely contradictory; and so they are, but that is not the
point. What is important is the character of their transforming inter-
action, and I would suggest that the few clues that do exist concerning
this are contained in the passages of Scripture available to us. Not that
we can expect to find in the teachings of Christ a comprehensible programme of action or even a pattern of logic related to everyday experience, for they can only be taken to be intricate riddles about political
nonsense, that reveal truth only in so far as risks are taken on their
behalf. That is to say, spiritual truth is the converse in practice of
political logic.

I believe this to be the key to any understanding of the difficulties we
have variously encountered. There is a very real sense in which political
logic on the left (or the right for that matter) is little more than the rules
of a metamorphosis game. Like Dan's history, these are rules written
by the winners for the losers, to ensure that the winners always win and
the losers always lose even if the faces change. We dissent, of course,
but not from the game, and we accept that the only way to win
is to create a new loser to take our place. Conversely, the spiritual
dimensions we have simply taken as a subversion of enemy structures,

in fact undermine equally the presupposed theory and practice of our own struggle. The Holy Spirit is indeed subversive of armed capital, but do we really take it as being equally subversive of Marxism-Leninism? Or anarcho-pacifism?

From this side of the gaming table, it would seem that the movement of the spirit puts *all* the players into a state of extreme agitation. There is a flurry of manoeuvres as we attempt to deal with this heresy: to win is to lose the game and to lose is finally to win all. Very few of us are able to take our eyes from the state of play for long enough to decode what in fact is an elaborate and obscure message about total revolution in the revolution. Just as the apocalpytic fantasies of John are codified messages about belief in a bad time, so the gospels are codified messages about turning the world and everything in it, including ourselves, upside down. John's messages were designedly incomprehensible to the Special Branch of his time and, in a similar way, the gospels are to be taken as incomprehensible except in practice. As a piece of intellectual logic or political theory they are a bad joke – they have to be done to be believed.

For a brief period, this event flashed a number of extraordinary images at us, allowing us a fleeting glimpse of a truly alternative Christian community. It was rich and it was stimulating, and it provided what many of us feared had vanished without trace – the possibility that we could allow joy to break out of control and envelop our sterile politicking. It was perhaps a confirmation of each other and a confirmation that all was indeed not lost. But we were reminded yet again that anything we create as an alternative to the dark grey institutions must, at the same time, actively disrupt their neat patterns of injustice. An alternative that does not engage the original horror, thereby opening the possibility of alternatives for further victims, is only an indulgence of special opportunities – a new privilege. The sword must be two-edged and it must not bring peace, we are told. So I would like to introduce another image, an image that is also a paradox, of the two-edged sword of the gospel; an image that has also been taken by Roel Van Duyn to intimate the role of the Amsterdam Kabouters. It is the symbol of the peacock butterfly who flutters splendidly and eagerly with its beautiful bright wings. 'Love and co-operation are its normal mode of life. If a predator approaches it opens out its wings so that the predator is suddenly confronted with great menacing eyes, gazing intently in its direction. And the predator retreats. In the peacock butterfly affection and aggression are one. Love and aggression, the power of attraction and repulsion, carry it through life and death.' This is neither violence nor non-violence, if you will permit me further to muddy the water, and it is certainly a mistake to be turning the other cheek as a strict rule of political practice, for a further illogicality of the gospel is that there are no strict rules of practice. We are simply invited to confuse the enemy and risk our well-being. The rest is up to us to discover as we engage the Beast in ceremonial combat.

This is the stuff, and literally the non-sense, of the spiritual dimension. It cannot be communicated as a coherent, let alone viable, way of going on in any accepted political sense and yet there are occasions when we know it to be a decisive factor in our struggle. For most of the time it is subdued beneath our panic-ridden lives, our tearing inhibitions, and yet there are occasions when we can become quite disturbed by its capacity to undermine our defence mechanisms. Despite our hard-bitten interiors, I believe we allowed these four days to be just such an occasion, leaving us flushed and excited and in a state of great confusion. I suspect that those who were there have had the greatest difficulty giving a credible answer to the inevitable question: what came out of the conference?

Nevertheless, for an instant, we saw, and having seen, believed. And for us, the struggle can never be quite the same again; we clearly cannot return to our meagre visions as if nothing out of the ordinary had occurred. Neither, however, can we assume that the event has provided us with a clear way forward, a programme of action, a kind of post-Huddersfield package deal that puts all our problems in a nutshell for a once-over cracking. (It is crucial we understand this, for the simple solution is the refuge of Stalinists and evangelicals, and is another face of the Beast.) There is a certain disorder of the soul as an inevitable mark of the Spirit, opening us to wholly new possibilities all with their attendant price tags. We are free to buy or to turn away, but we can no longer pretend that for us, the offer has not been made. In many ways, of course, the possibilities are unattractive in the extreme, exposing our lives to great danger or even insecurity, and the wisest counsel is undoubtedly caution; while the counsel of our unwise faith is always to throw caution (like seeds) to the wind, risking all for the chance of life.

In our inner selves and in our communities we can do no more now than risk all for the chance of life and liberation.

Thomas Cullinan
WHERE THE EUCHARIST TAKES OFF

'I want to celebrate my God for no reason at all' (Ivan Illich). We did just that.

As a Catholic monk I found it hard to get under the skin of those who wanted to be radical, serious, political and spiritual to boot by off-loading all the baggage picked up from the past. I wondered what they meant by being 'trapped again in the straight-jacket of institutional religion'. A few years ago Mario Borelli, from Naples, spoke in Oxford and at the end a voice shouted, 'And just what is the church doing to help you?' He laughed. 'That is a very English question, I *am* the church.' Just how do we draw that convenient distinction, so easy for linguistic or polemical reasons, between an institution and a living community of faith, a living tradition? If we get up-tight about the skeleton, and do away with it, we must not be surprised if the heart, the flesh, the warmth, the life, atrophy and die.

I suppose as a monk I am by vocation *marginal*, called to live on the edge as a critic of institutionalism while related to the institution. But there are times of real anger, anger at the greed of so much of our economy (we like to call it growth), anger at the innate violence, the structural injustice, the manipulation of people, anger with the blindness of my own monastic community at times. Then I want to throw up everything, fly like a bird to a mountain, escape and be innocent and free. But then humour and humility and honesty take over; I know that all I have is a gift, even my ability to stand aside, contemplate and criticize. I know that gifts are for sharing and serving, not for possessing. I know that much of the gift, my faith, my vision, my longings are given largely through history. I am within a tradition of faith and generosity, a wild and wonderful tradition, sinful and saintly, needful and wheatful, a tradition stretching back and embraced by God's Son for whom good and evil could no more be separated than goodies and baddies. And when I am *really* honest I know that I have within me the seeds of every beastliness the world has ever brought forth – as well as the seeds of liberation.

I arrived at Huddersfield with a little bread and a flask of wine, expecting to celebrate mass in a corner with a handful of students or whoever. But it became clear that things would not be so. Lurking in disguise among those at the conference were all sorts of chaplains, seminarians, missionaries and others, lined up to celebrate God in the eucharist. And Dan Berrigan made it plain that it was just that eucharist which had crystallized the faith of their small prison group, transforming mere resistance into Christian hope and vision.

So we celebrated, on the Saturday, eighty of us jammed into the billiard room, singing to guitars, subversive prayer, saying again the words, 'This is my body, this my blood, poured for you and for all.' A simple eucharist, catching the mood and the theme of the conference, the sense of political urgency and the yearning for spiritual depth. Both of these seemed to be caught by that ancient myth of bread and wine which carries us far out beyond the limited horizons of our own categories of thought; that mystical statement of faith which commits us to a political view of man far more radical than most of those who 'attend mass' would care to admit; a political statement about what it is for men to be called to freedom, what it is for men to be called into communion with each other (finding its term in God far beyond mere togetherness), what it is for men to have things or money or power in their control (finding their origin in God – these are for sharing and not for possessing), what it means to be totally embedded in the here-and-now struggle, yet always to have hope and joy (because in spite of all it is God's world and he has not lost control); above all it is a political statement because unequivocally it celebrates that good is more powerful than evil, non-violence than violence, truth than the manipulation of power.

The word got around, and on Sunday there were 120 or so. The priest whom I asked to preside said he was not sure how to cope with this sort of thing. Well, none of us was; it took off somewhere between the readings and the songs, and none of us was quite in control. For the first time I realized that the eucharist will be the means of drawing Christians into a living community of faith and hope, not merely an expression of what unity already exists. We pray that those who eat this one bread, drink this one cup, may be drawn into the one body of Christ.

We exchanged the kiss of peace, with that strange Christian sense of joy which is so close to suffering, the blood of death and the bread of life shattering our nice categories. God's ways are not ours, his peace tears us to bits. And it all ended with the guitarists from Dublin leading off down the sabbath-quiet streets of Huddersfield with 120 people singing.

The itch was strong, and on the Monday, in spite of urgent pressures to get cleared up and away, we celebrated once again. This time we found ourselves dancing too, for ours is a dancing God. When God no longer dances and when God no longer tears men to pieces, men have lost their vision and their hope.

Basil Moore
COMMUNITY AND RESPONSE

The SCM Conference at Huddersfield had a theme and a list of speakers. The theme 'Spiritual Dimensions of Political Involvement' attracted a number of people who were in search of 'spiritual sustenance'. At the same time the impressive array of speakers, with an impressive record of political involvement, attracted a number of people in search of a political dimension to their committed Christian lives.

The conference did little to enlighten the Christian's political pursuit. Little time and fewer words were spent on political analysis or planning. This did not seem to upset people unduly.

Predictably, a good deal more time was spent on the question and in acts of worship. It cannot be denied by even the most sceptical of critics that for many the acts of worship were profoundly disturbing and enriching experiences. Yet, not very much was done to lay a solid foundation beyond inspiration for the continuance of this experience. No one seemed unduly perturbed about this either.

What had become a reality in the conference was a sense of community, of joy, of co-operation. This reality took over from the hot questions with which we had arrived. Perhaps, in this experience, our different questions were being answered in a three-dimensional way. 'Community' was sensed as the answer to our search for personal and spiritual support in our political involvement, as much as it was sensed as the starting point for radical political action. Let us examine this a little more closely.

A major criticism that has been levelled at a conference like this, and at the commune movement generally, is that it is a way of opting out: it is entering into a way of living so different from the life style of the masses of the people that it is politically impotent: it is a way of escaping from the oppressions which the ordinary person faces.

There is obviously truth in this. Conferences can be pleasant holiday experiences which make no fundamental differences to our 'back home' situations. Some communes may have been extended 'holiday conferences'. But this does not mean that communes are inherently political dead ends.

One way of looking at politics is to see it as a way in which we act to defend our own life style – i.e. going beyond where we are at, in order to give where we are at some stability.

It is easy to see the politics of 'extended self-interest' at work in international capitalism. Here the supreme value is individual competition, with wealth and power as the co-terminus goal. The victors in this game will never willingly surrender their rewards. There is no evidence of the political potency of altruism. In fact, to surrender the rewards would undermine the competitive game itself. The logical and inevitable result of a competitive society is an unequal society. This inequality creates enormous social tensions and potential revolutions. To protect themselves the social bosses have to create hosts of substructure safeguards, including the advertising campaigns for consumerism and the nuclear family. Because of all these subtle pressures the forces of conservatism permeate society, making it inordinately difficult to dislodge the powered élite. Most of us do not really wish to rid our society of the possibility of a powerful, rich élite. We would prefer to have their wealth and power and so to change the names of the people at the top.

On the political left of this pervasive, competitive status quo is a long, straggling, sprawling array of people and organizations. Tragically, down this span there is little that is truly subversive of the competitive sport. It is not that there are no alternative ideas or values. Nor is it that there is no ideological and emotional commitment. It is rather that there is very little in the life-style of the 'left' that distinguishes it from the life-style of the 'right'. This is especially true of the middle-class 'left', the predominant form of the 'left' encountered in the student world. The middle-class 'right' knows that it has little, if anything, to fear from the middle-class 'left' because, when the chips are down, they know that most of us will act to defend our life-style (including property, homes, business, shares, etc.) rather than the political noises we might have been making.

The call to communal living is a call to us to make a political statement with our lives; it is a call to 'have all things in common'; to share all our resources of time, energy, talents, money and goods. It is to eradicate as far as we can from our community the corroding value of competition, and to replace it with the integrating values of co-operation and consensus.

When and if that sort of co-operative, sharing, communal living becomes our life-style we will soon come to know that we can expect no unsolicited help from our competitive neighbours. Then the struggle for our continued existence will be on in earnest. We will not be impervious either from within ourselves or from without to the allure of the values that sustain the capitalistic edifice. Thus unless we evangelize (= policitize) beyond our own immediate circle, and do so successfully, the most likely consequence will be either that we are dismissed as innocuous freaks, or forced by both internal and external pressures to conform or quit.

The implication of this is that what gives both conservative and radical political action their strength, is that the people involved are also fighting for *themselves*. What distinguishes them are the life-styles being defended. In this sense, then, the alternative life-style of the commune, so far from being necessarily a way of opting out of political involvement should be a solid foundation of radical politics.

If the alternative, communal life-style can and should be the basis for radical political action, it can be argued that it can and should be the basis of deeply subversive worship.

There is a long list of eminently reputable sociologists who support the thesis that the function of religious ritual is to socialize the devotees as 'good citizens'. Whether we accept this or not, the fact remains that there is an uncomfortable parallel between most predominant theological theories and social and political structures in given situations. It is also true that for most, worship, instead of being a profoundly disturbing and radicalizing experience, is very comforting. When, and if, we have been radicalized, it has usually been through experiences outside the context of Christian worship.

This has created a deep dilemma. Many, as a result, have quit Christianity and long since ceased to participate in Christian worship. Others have clung tenaciously, but awkwardly, to Christianity. This has produced the welter of 'experimental' services we have witnessed over the past few years. Some of these have been purely gimmicky. Many more have tried to feed into the language, music and activity of the services vision of the alternative society. The uncomfortable truth, however, is that these radical experiments have not really been radicalizing or socializing experiences.

In its worship the conservative, competitive 'community' has been able to offer up its life-style to God, and in that act to find it reinforced. On the other hand, the radicals have given their worship a radical content, not a radical context. Our worship, as a result, has been neither truly subversive, nor sustaining – and it has certainly not been socializing.

If there is any truth in the sociologists' thesis of the social significance of religious ritual, then in worship we should be offering up to God a total life style, and in the offering find our experience deepened, challenged and reinforced. Is it not possible that it is our schizophrenic love/

hate relationship with our own competitive, individualistic and privileged life-style that makes our worship (both in its conservative and radical variety) a barren and deeply alienating experience for us? We are ashamed of our life-style, and dislike its religious reinforcement. Since, however, we are not making any deeply convinced and convincing statement with our *lives*, we are unable to make such statements in our worship. Try as hard as we like, when what we *do* clashes so deeply with who we *are*, our worship not infrequently ends up as simply embarrassing.

Radical worship, like radical politics, thus springs from the same seed – the living experience of a truly sharing and co-operative human community. Is it not possible that it is this for which Paul argued so passionately in his letter to the Corinthians (cf. especially 1 Cor. 11–13)?

We have talked so far about community and political action, and community and worship. Deeper than both of these, however, is the need for sustaining inter-personal relations. If nothing else succeeds in driving us into a vital Christian community, this may.

Perhaps the group in Britain and Ireland that feels most keenly a depressing loneliness and isolation, is the group of people represented at Huddersfield – the disaffected students, post-graduates, teachers, religious and social workers. It is this group more than any other that finds it so difficult to find any 'purchase' in our society. We know that by birth, family, education and social history we belong to the 'middle class', or at least we have a ticket to the front positions in the competitive race which we can choose either to use or to refuse to use. When we choose not to use them, we are immediately isolated from our 'natural' community with whom we could be expected to be working for the preservation of the status quo. When we try to get onto the right side of the struggle for change in our society, we are both deeply embarrassed by not being 'working class', and not really able to feel comfortably and rewardingly 'at home' in the milieu that has no ticket to wealth, power, position and prestige. We know on whose side we would like to be fighting, but do not know how to root ourselves so deeply on that side that we are fighting our own rather than 'their' battle.

In this thinly populated zone we desperately need sustaining human relationships, without which we will be drained of energy, vision and ideas. And this zone is thinly populated primarily because we don't really inhabit it. We populate the privileged zone and ease our conscience with radical noises.

Our real difficulty is not how to become 'working class', and the sickly paternalism of offering help to the 'working class' is simply not on. Our need is to create a deeply committed alternative life-style which, as an alternative, draws us into the political arena on our own behalf, seeking allies in the struggle for change.

Here again, in our search for deeply sustaining interpersonal relationships, we are driven to the radically committed, communal, co-operative, sharing community, which, at the same time, we have argued is the basis for transforming political action and worship.

It is not politically subversive activity that is needed, it is the seed-bed in which radical Christian action can grow with authentic strength. It is not subversive worship that we need, because our worship will not be subversive, no matter what its language, until it grows out of and enriches a life-style that in itself says 'no' to competition, privilege and inequalities of power and wealth. And, being who we are, we will need each other desperately to survive. We need a community of people whose lives are dominated by the values of co-operation and sharing in all things.

Thus, perhaps, the seeds of liberation will be found only in the content of our living, rather than in fine political or theological statements, or strange 'experimental' acts of worship. If so, we should not be surprised. It was Jesus who said that the truth which would set us free is a 'doing' rather than a 'knowing'.

The real question remains; will we have the courage to change the context of our living?

Mary Condren
CELIBACY AND THE
LIBERATION OF WOMEN

The only difference between the position of women in society and the position of women in the church is that the latter is seldom talked about, and even where it is, support for the present attitudes towards this species will be forthcoming from all angles, as the church puts its philosophical weight on the rubber stamp it uses to endorse the status quo. For centuries the co-operation of the churches has been the mainstay of the state, either in an absorptionist or abstentionist sense. Whenever it has reared its head in opposition to the state, it has seldom been for any other reason than a threat to its own power. Its attitude to the sexual status quo has either been complete acquiescence or reaction defined by the nature of the status quo at the time. It is my belief that this state of affairs has had serious consequences for the church, especially in the realm of sexuality. Roles have been defined and clearly delineated so that the unique freedom of Christ in relation to women and children has been cut short at every level. It is ironic that the only acceptable nude male figure in our society is the image of Christ on the cross. Christ himself has become an opiate for use by those oppressed by their position in the wider society, and also I would maintain by their counterparts within the church itself.

Dotted all over the countryside are what I would call 'spiritual harems', communities of women founded on the male models with systems of authority and rules made as often to protect the inmates from intrusion as for any positive functions based on the gospel of Christ. The rules and regulations, etc., are in the main taken from the constitutions of the male religious orders. Adaptations and changes are made by male Canonical Visitors, male retreat masters, male confessors, male preachers, male brothers in the order and male superiors in the order ... sometimes with the consent of the female inhabitants. The result of all this is that where the young idealist has not committed psychological suicide as an offering to the maintenance of the religious status quo, she will have been saved in spite of, rather than because of, this system of religious crucifixion.

Herein lie the voodoo dolls, providing the spiritual strength to those in the battlefield (i.e. mission fields near and far). 'We priests rely on your prayers to give us the grace to carry on. We too would like to lead your lives of prayer but we have had to sacrifice this kind of life to work in the vineyards.' Strangely reminiscent, is it not, of your average husband? 'I'd just love to be sitting here at home all day doing nothing. You ought to come and work in the factory and see what it is like.' And like your average husband, when these same priests were given an opportunity to live a contemplative life for one or two year periods in a special retreat house, it had to close within a few years through lack of support. But the saga continues as they make their visitations, making rules they will never keep themselves, letter censoring, no television (except for important things like moon landings or the Pope's coronation), the list is endless. Or on the other hand you may have the so-called liberal approach. 'Yes, you may shorten your skirts, and show your hair, and go to the theatre and live in flats, but for God's sake don't rock the boat, the older sisters cannot take any more, they too must be considered.' (In fact they are often the most radical.) In short, you may have all the illusions of change, modernize (i.e. conform to the standards set by the machine), but beyond that you may not go, otherwise you risk losing all the 'spiritual privileges' of your religious state. Apart from the usual indulgences and share in the countless prayers and masses said for religious, these privileges include social, medical, housing security and all the other benefits which have accrued to you through your vow of poverty. If the education system has had any success with you at all, it is unlikely that you will take this risk, quite apart from the fact that one's emotional life has been channelled in entirely different directions, idealized, absolutized. This is true both of men and women who leave, for whatever reason, their religious states.

So the role of nuns in the church, apart from the social first aid activities which have been passed over almost entirely to them, is a spiritual one. In addition to this they may spend their lives making the antiquated vestments some priests still insist on wearing; the 'religious objects' some priests insist on handing out, betraying as often their own principles in deference to the 'wishes of the faithful'; and building up the double-standard existence which is their lot. You will also find them doing the odds and ends that no commercial firm would touch, such as religious habits, special communion bread, pietistic artwork, altar cloths and other objects used to delineate the sacred from the secular – all adding up to the fact that one of the main props of the religious 'other world' is based on the exploitation of women, who, in deference to a male dominated theological understanding, nevertheless consider it to be a privilege.

'The newsletter of the South African Dutch Reformed Church makes interesting reading sometimes. A report of the Synod's discussion about women in the church "reaffirmed that it is the teaching of Scripture that women be excluded from the office of ruling preaching ... However, women should not be excluded from the work of the church." So the Synod recommends to the member churches that they "make full use of the gifts and services of women in the diaconal services in auxiliary capacities and in appropriate teaching situations"' (*Roadrunner*, Issue 42). Amazing, isn't it, and yet before you go into a shock coma, let me remind you that this is exactly the position of women in our own churches here today. It is only in the last year or two that women in the Vatican were doing anything other than washing the Pope's socks and serving him breakfast ... not to mention cleaning the floors and other womanly tasks. Women in the Catholic church are still prohibited from reading at services, whilst their traditional serving role is performed here by small boys. Women are only allowed into the sanctuary during a service when they are getting married. God knows why, and he's not telling anyone! Of course they may go in at other times to clean the candlesticks, flower decorations, and for general scrubbing up. Apart from that you will find them in every seminary as kitchen drudges, in every presbytery as priests' housekeepers, and ... if you have really made it ... you might be allowed to type the parish magazine. I once asked an Indian whether they had any nuns in India. 'No,' he replied, 'only priest's wives.'

Despite its reverent nods of the Virgin Mary, the institutional church has clearly decided that the liberation promised to all 'men' by the redemption of Christ, from the sins of Adam and Eve, clearly does not extend to women, who must be kept down for fear of a repeat performance of the apple saga. I once suggested to a priest of the order to which I belonged that it might be possible for us to work together on a particular project. My vocation was seriously in doubt when I made it clear that I saw our role as other than washing priests' underwear!

It may be clear from the remainder of this article that I speak from the rare perspective of having been immersed in church structures for some time. I would want to point out, however, that my criticisms are in no way directed at the institutions of celibacy as such. Freely chosen, celibacy and virginity can have the greatest consequences for the people of God as a whole. By 'freely chosen' I mean understood in all its consequences, psychological and social, for just as there can be no sin without understanding, likewise with virtue. I am concerned, however, with the fact that in the Catholic church at least, the ideal of commitment to working towards the kingdom has become synonymous with virginity, and where Vatican 2 may have changed things on paper, there are still generations of religious formed in the old mould who are going to be around for a long time.

The consequences of a virginity which is based on the celibate literalism applied to the Virgin Birth, can and has had the most disastrous consequences. Rather than the freeing of a person to radical work for the kingdom, or the proleptic living out of loving relationships towards all, instead of narrowly confining it in the nuclear family set-up; or the ability to stand outside the structures of society 'at the edge' to provide a permanent revolutionary stance, celibacy and virginity have been degraded to mean an absence of sex and the worship of a deaf idol. The consequences are evident. In the male models we have the 'straining of gnats and the swallowing of camels and the attendant theological nit-picking of a guilt-ridden syndrome'. The female will 'naturally' express this in the furious cleansing of souls and body and the polishing of floors, till the convent is more like a skating rink. One evening as a young nun, newly professed, I was walking up the staircase after Compline. It was about nine in the evening and as I looked out the window (the practice is discouraged) I could see behind the autumn golden red mature leaves, a blazing sun showering its last defiant rays before the night closed in. The sky was lit up in a phantasy of colours all witnessing (as I thought then) to the beauty of God's creation. I met a sister at the top of the stairs. 'Look,' she said, pointing to the window. 'Yes,' I replied, 'isn't it beautiful.' 'What is beautiful?' she asked. I told her about the sun and sky and the leaves and the trees. 'Look at the windows,' she demanded. So I narrowed my gaze and peered, still not knowing what she meant until she said, 'I only washed them yesterday and look there are flymarks all over them.' I finally squinted my eyes and yes, I could see the traces of the guilty fly. Suddenly I grew all hot and angry and told her once again about the trees and the sky and the leaves and the sun. 'It's all right for you to talk, just wait until you have to wash those windows, then you will see the flymarks too.' I think it was then that I understood, and knew that I could never wash those windows.

This episode summed up all my latent fears, the narrowing, the compression, the tailoring, and it burned inside me until one day I shouted, 'Look, this gospel of Christ, was this not about freedom of the spirit?' 'Yes, but of course it was, *spiritual* freedom,' to which I could give no reply. It became clear that the Jesus I had come to know through (ironically, meditation and study of the scripture), was a relation to the Jesus of the institutional church, who had long since been elevated, obscured, mystified and enthroned out of harm's way, while the old authoritarian God was still reigning and it was our job to spend our lives pacifying him on behalf of a wicked world.

I have less experience of the effects of celibacy on male orders, but I am tempted to think that the four-letter jokes at which they are brilliant are an unhealthy sign. In addition to this there is their attitude to women, which is a great revelation to someone on hearing it for the first time. There are the typical sad jokes about Mother's Unions, Women's Sodalities, Legion of Mary and nuns. One that goes the rounds is about a young priest who said mass in a particular convent for the first time. Afterwards two nuns came and talked with him while he ate his breakfast, a boiled egg. When he had finished the nuns asked him what he wanted for breakfast the following morning. 'I will have two eggs and one nun.' Yes, I know it's not very funny, but in the clerical circles where it is usually related they find it hilarious. I think it is sad, but not half so sad as the pictures of the same clerics in all the religious weeklies, etc., in the centre of groups of about 500 women leading them on a pilgrimage or other worthy cause. Some day I will write a poem about someone who refused to submit to the sexual crucifixion that society imposed on him as an offering to its new-found idol and quietly slipped away from the milling crowds. I think he wanted to pray.

Society will always have its people who suffer or are good on its behalf to set standards and maintain tensions. Yet just as we can no longer be uncritical appendages to the economic status quo, so too with the sexual, in a positive rather than an abstentionist sense. The church's acquiescence to the institution of the nuclear family has meant a serious loss and diversion of potential energy and full-time commitment to the liberation or redemptive movement. Children have entered the realm of private property, and so a full-time keeper must be attached to their growth (inevitably the woman), leaving the male (or middle-class woman who can afford a nanny) to get on with their job of making the values of humanness subservient to those of efficiency and expansion and 'law and order'. Virginity then is the only alternative to this for most women – an extreme price to pay, and the support for which must then be forthcoming from such aberrations as 'Sisters of the Divine Infant' or 'Bride of Christ', etc. In our new Christian communities or communes which must go hand in hand with the liberation and women and children, we who 'have risen from the dead with Christ' might at last come to some idea of what Christ was on about when he said 'when they rise from the dead, men and women do not marry; no, they are like the angels in heaven'. Likewise, when celibacy becomes a *real* option, it will no longer 'prove God's transcendence, rather the whole being will express it' (Illich). Hence, women's liberation is not merely a peripheral concern but a vital part of liberating our structures and theology from the patriarchal stranglehold that is now on them. Theologians and scripture scholars should all be tickled to death, leaving us free to deal with the wider strangleholds that the patriarchal state places on all its subjects.

Alistair Kee
CHRISTIAN RESISTANCE IN BRITAIN

None of the main contributions deals directly with Britain, and there is a danger that we might fail to benefit from them, by allowing our attention to be taken up with details of what is happening in the United States or in Namibia. Eventually the question must be faced, What does all this mean for us in Britain today? In particular, How does all this bear on the problem of spiritual dimensions to political struggle? While neither the model of Southern Africa nor that of the United States provides us with an answer, inevitably the American situation is closer to our own. The contributions of Dan Berrigan and Jim Forest have presented us with a very clear possibility and challenge.

The radical tradition in politics has tended to be issue-oriented. Issues or problems are identified and strategies and tactics worked out to deal with them. The situation which I described in 'The Criticism of the Spirit' is one in which radical Christians have joined the radical political tradition, have accepted the issues and even many of the strategies and tactics. The question then arises, Is there any distinctively Christian contribution to all this? Such a contribution has been difficult or impossible to identify. At the same time, failure to resolve the issues has led to frustration and resignation. In Britain we have almost an entire generation of disillusioned radicals who have grown weary trying to win battles over their particular issues, from CND to a free bus service.

What came through from the American contributions was that although a movement began with an issue, viz., the war in Vietnam, resistance to the war spread out as the implications of the warfare state became clearer. Resistance which had begun as resistance to an issue, became much more positive as it developed into a life style, resistant to the whole range of social seductions and cultural distractions. One striking comment was that over the years, the only resistance groups which had continued and gone on were not only Christian, but eucharistic. Individuals who go it alone are picked off, isolated and finally led to conform again. But even among the groups which have been set up, those which continue have had a spiritual centre to them. This is the possibility and the challenge which we must now face in Britain.

Christian resistance seems to present a very positive way of coming at the problem of spiritual dimensions to political struggle. A resistance group or community is aware of the issues of the day, indeed may have been set up originally in response to one particular issue. But the life of the group is not that of reacting to issues. The true 'reactionaries', in political terms, may be those who only react to issues, without offering a radical alternative which would eliminate both the issues and their causes. The resistance is not geared to an issue, and yet it also responds to issues, so that it is not a romantic or aesthetic alternative, such as we see in some groups which withdraw to remote parts of the Scottish highlands. But when we ask about the Christian contribution, there are two obvious areas.

The first concerns the nature of the resistance community. No matter how it first came into being, its life does not depend on dealing with a particular issue: above all, it does not depend on solving the problem or winning a particular struggle. The life of the group has a deep spiritual centre, and it is nourished not by tactical sessions, but by eucharistic occasions and by study of the Bible. This is the first contribution, that the life of the group is sustained from its spiritual depth. The importance of this is that groups which depend on solving issues or winning battles eventually collapse when the issues are not solved or the battles won. But the Christian resistance group is not 'reactionary' in this sense, and can bear the long haul.

The second contribution which Christian resistance makes to the spiritual dimensions to political struggle is that the life of the community may well enable the members to develop a distinctive view of what the real issues are, and how they can best be tackled. To put it briefly, it looks as if the Christian resistance in America is more subversive both in the short- and long-term than any merely political group – more subversive of the social and political life-style of America as we know it. This throws light on the impasse experienced among radical Christians in Britain. We may too easily have accepted the agenda and the tactics already agreed by the politicos. The specifically Christian contribution to political struggle may well begin by Christians appearing to go their own way, learning to do their own thing first. From time to time they may find themselves acting alongside non-Christians on particular issues, even doing the same thing. But the fundamental contribution will be a developing of an alternative life which is not only sustained from a spiritual depth, but which is also a sharp critique of the political situation. The criticism of the spirit, as was already noted, falls on the political as well as the religious.

It is in this direction that we are challenged by the resistance movement in America. There may be people in Britain working along these lines already, and we need to learn from each other. Eucharistic groups have started to meet in two or three places in Britain, in response to the presentations of Dan Berrigan and Jim Forest. It is much too early yet to say how they will develop, and above all whether they will be able to stand the pressures to give up and conform. These pressures come from all around, not least from the church. But we have made a start. We are not at all sure what we are getting into, except that it is what we should be getting into. For many of us, it is something that we have been looking for for some time, yet something which we fear very much. We have decided not to be drawn too quickly into political or even social activism again. The main objective at this moment is to gather strength and gain depth to our life together, through meeting, letting the Bible speak to us in our new situation, through celebrating this new life and through passing the bread and sharing the wine. Those who are continuing to worship regularly Sunday by Sunday find that this experience has given worship new significance. For those of us who no longer find any reality in such worship, it has given us a way of expressing the deep things of our Christian faith and finding renewal and strength.

It is as though for a short time we have withdrawn from the struggle, but we hope that when we are more confident we shall be able to pursue it in a more realistic way than before. We are aware of the danger, that we shall become so caught up in the life of the group that we shall never emerge from it. There is the danger that we shall always be preparing ourselves for an obedience which never comes. But this risk must be taken, for unlike the political groups to which we might otherwise belong, we recognize that we ourselves are part of the enemy in the struggle. Whatever it is that we must resist, we shall discover that we are involved in it, and contribute to its strength and perpetuation. We must get ourselves together in order to see what we are about.

Developing a Christian life together has become a priority in carrying on the struggle. We have all belonged to Christian groups which functioned as talk shops. At the present moment the obstacle is not lack of information, but lack of obedience; not lack of ideas, but of courage; not lack of clarity, but of faith. Whatever the religious meaning of the cross, it is a sign of trouble, and those who take up the cross are in trouble.

Christian life together has become a priority also over against the political groups. They may be talk shops and/or activist groups, but what has become clear is that they do not see their own involvement in the evil they oppose. Beyond that, they do not embody or exemplify the life that they proclaim. After the event (revolution) all will be new – and it never is. It seems certain that such groups simply reinforce the evil structures of the world. As Dan Berrigan might say, the Beast recognizes another beast. In our Christian tradition, however, we are promised an earnest, a first instalment now, of the life of the gospel. This suggests why the political groups in America have collapsed, while the eucharistic groups have continued. Political groups live in the anticipation of a victory which they rarely achieve. It may be that the eucharistic groups already live from a victory which gives them new life. They may not win battles and things may even get worse, but they experience in adversity the victory they proclaim.

And the Christian life together is a priority also within the life of the church. The church is often referred to as the Body of Christ, but in practice it does not embody Christ. It has no corporate life bearing the marks of Christ, of prophetic judgment, acceptance, forgiveness, joy, sacrifice, humility, hope, love, etc. Since the church is not constituted for such corporate life it seems necessary to develop communities precisely for this end. But to speak of communities within the church may raise the question of that great alternative, the monastic tradition of spirituality. In its greatest examples does it merely condemn us for continuing to live within our societies? From America we are reminded of the contribution of Thomas Merton. It is not a question of developing a monastic community, but of asking those who pursue this vocation – yet remaining in touch with the modern world – what perspective it gives them, which could assist us in our life and witness.

This is one possible response to the contributions of Dan Berrigan and Jim Forest. It is too early to say how it will grow or continue, but it does seem to speak directly to those who are concerned with spiritual dimensions to political struggle. It suggests a way of being true to the deep things of our faith, while bringing them to bear on the issues which rightly stir us.

NOTES ON CONTRIBUTORS

DANIEL BERRIGAN s.j.

'The first generation of Jesuits worked in the streets; the second generation bought a house; the third air-conditioned it. I belong to the first generation . . .'

Fr Daniel Berrigan – poet, priest, war resister and fugitive from injustice – is certainly the best known American Jesuit of any generation. He began hitting headlines in 1965 when he appeared at a memorial service for Roger La Porte, a young Catholic Worker who had immolated himself in protest against the Vietnam war. Daniel's refusal to condemn the act led to an outraged hierarchy expelling him from the United States to Mexico. Some ten thousand prominent Catholics responded with a full page ad in the New York Times protesting his exile and demanding his return. He was back two months later, further radicalised by his experiences in Latin America, and planning a ferocious all-out resistance to the war. The following three years of speaking, preaching, marching and organizing brought Daniel, his brother Philip and seven other Catholic revolutionaries to a point of desperation. If the war was to be stopped it would not be stopped by polite legal protest, and so:

Today, May 17th, we enter Local Board No. 33 at Catonsville, Maryland, to seize Selective Service records and burn them with napalm manufactured by ourselves from a recipe in the Special Forces Handbook, published by the U.S. Government. We, American citizens, have worked with the poor in the ghetto and abroad. We destroy these draft records not only because they exploit our young men, but because they represent misplaced power concentrated in the ruling class of America . . . We confront the Catholic Church, other Christian bodies and the synagogues of America with their silence and cowardice in face of our country's crimes. We are convinced that the religious bureaucracy in this country is racist, is an accomplice in war and is hostile to the poor . . . Now this injustice must be faced, and this we intend to do, with whatever strength of mind, body and grace that God will give us. May God have mercy on our nation.

It proved to be a prophetic act, electrifying the church, the peace movement and the new left, all of whom had in some way become locked into levels of complacency about the war. Soon, draft boards right across America were to be raided by priests, nuns, seminarians and plain ordinary Christians. *The war, they said, stops here.* Daniel Berrigan, for his part in the action, at Catonsville, was sentenced to three years imprisonment – a sentence which he decided he would not submit to voluntarily. For eight months Berrigan lived underground, hunted by the F.B.I., surfacing periodically to speak at rallies, writing prolifically to friends and enemies. It was the most celebrated act of defiance, turning half the Catholic church into co-conspirators (or at least accessories after the fact). It ended in the home of theologian William Stringfellow, when F.B.I. agents burst through the window finally to sieze their elusive priest.

That, it was generally assumed, was that. But in November 1970 came the sensational charge by F.B.I. Director J. Edgar Hoover that the Berrigan brothers, from inside Danbury prison, were behind a conspiracy to kidnap Henry Kissinger and to blow up the heating tunnels of government buildings! It was a mammoth lie, and was proved as such at the equally mammoth trial in Harrisburg which concluded with a hung jury.

Daniel Berrigan is the author of fifteen books of prose and poetry and a play, *The Trial of the Catonsville Nine*. His book, *The Dark Night of Resistance*, received the Frederick Melcher Award as well as the Thomas More medal for most distinguished work of Catholic literature published in 1971. Dan Berrigan was released last year on parole from Danbury Federal Prison.

COLIN WINTER

Colin Winter was born in 1928, is married and has five children. Born and educated in England he read theology at Oxford University and went to the theological seminary at Ely, Cambridge. Called to South Africa by Archbishop Joost de Blank, he was for several years rector of St Francis' Church Simonstown, a multi-racial parish near Cape Town. His book *Just People* deals with his years in Simonstown.

The people of Damaraland still regard him as their bishop although he was deported last year for his support of the Ovambo strikers. 'The British Embassy tried to tell me in rather bored terms that it was a strike for a few extra Rand. This is a lie, it wasn't. They were striking for the right to have their families with them; to choose their own employers; to have a say in the conditions under which they work; to move about as free men. The strike was really an effective "no" to apartheid.'

At present he is still carrying on the administration of the diocese of Damaraland as 'bishop-in-exile', whilst travelling continually to keep his peoples' cause before the eyes of the world.

JIM FOREST

Jim Forest, a leading Catholic radical in America, is currently working at the newly established Thomas Merton Life Centre which was founded by two nuns active in war resistance. He was a member of the 'Milwaukee Fourteen' who in 1968 broke into Selective Service Offices, seizing and burning 10,000 draft records – landing himself a four-year jail term. A founder member, with Merton and Dorothy Day, of the Catholic Peace Fellowship, he was led to the point of direct action because the peace movement at the time 'had acquired a dehumanizing bureaucratic atmosphere and all our means of protesting this insane war over four years had failed'. So it was that 'in seeking a lifestyle to match the Church's rhetoric' he was left with no other course of action.

For several years Jim Forest was a resident worker at Emmaus House in Harlem – a centre for hospitality, community action, study and worship that in the sixties constituted a vanguard of action for many Catholic radicals.

ALISTAIR KEE

Alistair Kee was born in Scotland and studied theology at Glasgow University before going to New York for three years. There he did his post-doctorate work whilst working at the same time in an East Harlem Protestant parish. He subsequently obtained an appointment to lecture in theology at the University College of Rhodesia. It was during his time there that the white rebellion started in 1965 and Alistair left Rhodesia when he felt the time had come when he could do no more.

Since then he has been lecturing at the University of Hull where he has been actively involved in student radical politics and was the author of the pamphlet which followed the 1968 sit-in. He spends much of his time travelling to groups throughout the country, including two years which he spent as a Montgomery Lecturer for the Christian Education Movement. His first book *The Way of Transcendence* was published in 1971, dealing with what is now his continuing concern: 'the problem of making Christian faith available to people who grow up in a secular culture which does not provide grounds for religious beliefs'.

BASIL MOORE

Born 1935. Methodist theologian who left his native South Africa with his wife and four young children in August 1972, after six months of a five year banning order. At the time of the banning (for 'furthering the aims of Communism') he had resigned as General Secretary of the University Christian Movement to become director of a theological correspondence course for the African Independent Churches Association. The effect of the banning made this, and a host of other jobs, impossible and he ended up as stock controller of a motor firm. Meanwhile the Government and police were receiving a great deal of support from their neighbours – they not only kept a close watch on their every move and saw to it they received no visitors, but also made living impossible for them as a family. After a series of incidents ranging from tiresome to gruesome they decided to get out, and came to London. He is now co-ordinating secretary of the SCM.

THOMAS CULLINAN

Clothed as a Benedictine monk at Ampleforth Abbey, York in 1955 at the age of twenty and took his final vows in 1959. He read Mathematics at Oxford and Philosophy and Theology at Ampleforth. He was ordained a priest in 1965 and although his main present commitment is to a monastic life of prayer in community, he is an active member of the Commission for International Justice and Peace and is also a member of Oxfam's Council of Management.

MARY CONDREN

Born in 1947 in Dublin, she was until the age of 14 in the hands of a convent school. After leaving school ('by mutual consent') she spent six years working in industry, advertising and management, and was 'on the point of becoming a capitalist whizz kid when the Spirit moved and I found myself in an enclosed contemplative order'. Almost three years and many sun-showers later she was back again looking for Godot, having seen resemblance in Jesus Christ and Thomas Merton, among others. She is currently studying sociology and theology at Hull University.

VIV BROUGHTON

Born 23.5.43. Mis-educated at Maidstone Technical School, then for three years an apprentice at the Royal Ordnance Factory, Woolwich.

A break with the War Office came after a year's agitation inside the factory as a member of the Committee of 100. Active then in music as a drummer with David Bowie, the Pretty Things and Rare Bird, leading to a brief association with Musical Gospel Outreach. Founder member of the radical Christian group CHURCH and of the subsequent magazine, 'Catonsville Roadrunner'. Now working for the Student Christian Movement while living at the Railton House Community in Brixton, South London where he has been involved in neighbourhood organizing for the past three years.